Worldview:
Implications for
Missionary work

Daniel R. Sánchez, Ph. D.

Worldview:
Implications for missionary work
Copyright Daniel R. Sanchez, 2013
Library of Congress

ISBN 978-0-9852842-9-9

For more information about this book and other resources and
training materials, or to contact the authors, please refer to the
Church Starting Network web site: www.churchstarting.net

ACKNOWLEDGEMENTS

I express gratitude to the following people who in one way or another encouraged and helped me in the task of writing this brief volume. Special thanks goes to Dr. David Suazo for inviting me to present these lectures at the Central American Evangelical Theological Seminary. This remarkable academic institution has produced many distinguished leaders for the ministry. For many years I have been aware of the educational ministry of this seminary and have met people who have served the Lord in most effective manners as a result of the preparation they received in this institution.

I am also indebted to many authors whose writings have contributed to my knowledge of the subject. These persons include Bassam Chedid, Levi De Carvalho, Pablo Deiros, Raúl Canizares, Gilberto Cavazos González, Justo González, Paul Hiebert, Charles Kraft, Nestor Medina, Donald Moore, Eugene Nida, James Sire, James Slack, William Smalley, Samuel Shahid, Ninian Smart, Ed Stetzer, Alan Tippett, Miguel de la Torre, Gailyn Van Rheenen, and others.

INTRODUCTION

An understanding of the people among whom we minister is an absolute necessity for Christian ministry. This understanding of the cultures of people holds importance in our efforts in communicating the gospel, for discipling people, training leaders, and establishing indigenous churches. An indispensable beginning place for this imperative understanding relates to the concept of the worldviews of the people. The subject of worldview which we approach is, therefore, a foundation for our understanding of the people and for our ministry among them.

The Apostle Paul did not employ the word "worldview." In his first letter to the Corinthians, however, he stressed the importance of understanding the backgrounds of each group in his efforts to guide them to an experience of salvation in Jesus Christ. He said: *"To the Jew I have become as a Jew that I might win Jews, to those who are under the law as under the law that I might win those who are under the law . . . "* (1 Cor 9:20). He explains his motivation for doing this: *"that I might by all means save some"* (v. 22).

Paul obviously applied this principle in his ministry. For example, in the synagogue at Antioch, the Apostle began his presentation of the message with a brief overview of the deliverance of Israel and the messages of the prophets. After this introduction he presented Christ as the fulfillment of these prophecies (Acts 13). In Athens, addressing a group of Gentiles, Paul began his presentation of the gospel with references to the altar with the inscription "To the unknown god" and quoted their own poets (Acts 17). In both cases Paul took into account the backgrounds of those he addressed in presenting the message in such a way that they could understand and relate to it.

Our motivation behind writing this book is similar to that of the Apostle Paul's. The selection of worldviews takes into account the different backgrounds that are found among the various people groups. After introducing the concept of worldview, this book focuses on animistic, syncretistic, theistic, and postmodern worldviews. In each case, suggestions are given on how best to present the gospel, disciple believers, and start churches in that particular context.

This book is the result of a series of lectures delivered at the Central American Evangelical Theological Seminary in Guatemala City, Guatemala. I deeply appreciate the opportunity to present these papers to a select group of doctoral candidates and the affirmation and suggestions I received from them.

I am aware that this subject is so vast that what I have achieved here is simply to present a brief introduction. My hope is that the issues I have presented, the suggestions for reflection, and the sources I have cited may encourage readers to do a more extensive and profound research of the entire field worldviews. May the Lord fill us with His grace and wisdom that we may be able to make a statement similar to the Apostle Paul's: "To him who is animistic (syncretistic, theistic, postmodern) I am like animist (syncretistic, theistic, and postmodern) that by all means I might save some."

Contents

CHAPTER 1
The Worldview Concept

I have been asked to present a series of lectures on worldviews. As you know, the subject is so vast that we need to select the worldviews that are most relevant to our environments and our ministries. It is also important to note that due to my secular as well as religious preparation, I will present these lectures from the perspective of the social sciences (especially anthropology) as well as missiology.[1]

My interest, therefore, is that we get a clearer understanding of the concepts related to worldview in general and to the worldviews of those to whom we minister. Further, we must consider the missiological implications of these concepts in relation to the different socio-cultural groups among whom we work or with whom we will work in the future. With this in mind, we begin our discussion with an attempt to define the term "worldview." With the definition in mind, we will focus on the characteristics of a worldview, its main functions, and its importance in cross-cultural work.

Definition of Worldview

Worldview can be understood as "the view of the cosmos." It comprises the lenses we use to help us interpret reality. Worldview provides a foundation of beliefs taken for granted (usually without question) that a people group uses to explain the realities they face in the universe."[2]

Charles Kraft defines worldview as "the set of suppositions (including values and commitments allegiances) underlying how people perceive and respond to reality."[3] He explains:

> A whole group (society) may chart its course according to a single map of reality . . . We call such a perception shared by a social group and we see that worldview as the core of a culture, functioning, on one hand, as the grid in terms of which reality is perceived, and, on the other, as that which provides guidelines a people's behavioral response to that perception of reality . . . . [4]

Paul Hiebert's definition of worldview includes: "The central suppositions, concepts and premises more or less widely shared by members of a culture or subculture."[5] He states:

> Our worldview assures us that what we see is the way things really are. Like glasses, worldview shapes how we see the world around us. They are what we look with and not what look at. And because people in other cultures have different worldviews, they see reality differently at even the most fundamental levels.... In short, our worldview is our basic map of reality and the map we use for living our lives."[6]

N. T. Wright defines worldview as "the grid through which humans perceive reality."[7] Norman Geisler says that "people do not see things as they are but as they appear to be through the colored glasses of their worldview."[8] These writers underscore the fact that people see and understand the world through the perspective of their worldviews.

James W. Sire defines worldviews as follows:

> A worldview is a commitment, a fundamental orientation of the heart, that can be expressed as a story or in a set of presuppositions (suppositions which may be true, partially true or entirely false) which we hold (consciously or subconsciously, consistently or inconsistently) about the basic constitution of reality, and that provides the foundation on which we live and move and have our being.[9]

As seen in these definitions, the suppositions, premises, and ideologies shared by the members of a socio-cultural group determine how they view and interpret the world in which they live. The expression which Hiebert uses "more or less widely shared," indicates that there may be some degree of diversity within the group regarding the shared suppositions or premises. Sufficient common ground, however, provides a sense of common identity and a spirit of collaboration within the ethnic group because they see things in much the same perspective.[10]

Types of Worldviews

The authors of books and articles that discuss worldviews use different categories for the different types of worldviews. In his book, *The Universe Next Door,* James W. Sire provides an overview of worldviews that underpin the way Western world people think. He shows how worldview determines how Western people think about themselves, other people, the natural world, and about God or ultimate reality. He further demonstrates and historically traces how their worldviews have resulted in a decomposition of the theistic worldviews, resulting in deism, naturalism, nihilism, existentialism, Eastern Mysticism, and the consciousness of the New Age.[11]

Gailyn Van Rheenen divides worldviews into four categories:

- Secular Worldview (which divides the world between the supernatural and natural areas and focuses almost exclusively on natural sphere)

- Animist Worldview (which believes in personal spiritual beings and impersonal forces that have power over the affairs of humans)

- Pantheistic Worldview (which perceives a penetrating essence defined as "god" fills the universe)

- Theistic Worldview (which presupposes that God created heaven and earth and continues to watch over the universe).[12]

These worldviews are seen basically from a theological perspective even though they deal with the cultural aspects of their contexts.

In his book, *Worldview: Crosscultural Explorations of Human Beliefs*, Ninian Smart, basically divides the concept of worldviews in terms of the regions of the world. He puts these worldviews into six categories:

- The Modern West, largely Christian in background though largely pluralistic in character, stretching from the American Pacific eastward through Europe to Siberia, and from Norway in the North to Armenia in the South

- The Islamic Crescent stretching from Indonesia westward to northern Nigeria in West Africa, via parts of South Asia to the Middle East, North Africa, and reaching northward into the former Soviet Central Asia

- South and much of Southeast Asia, all with a background of Indian-style civilization, comprising Tibet, India, Sri Lanka, Burma, Thailand, Laos, and Cambodia.

- East Asia, from China and Vietnam, via Korea and Japan, comprising the Chinese sphere of influence.

- The Latin South, from the Rio Grande to Patagonia.

- Black Africa and the Caribbean

- The Pacific region.[13]

Smart presents these worldviews in such a general manner that the reader receives an idea of their basic suppositions but lacks details about local contexts.

Obviously, the task of classifying worldviews is extremely difficult and complicated. This difficulty stems from the rapid changes that are happening in the world, the different perspectives from which they can be seen, and the large number of sub-worldviews that exist among peoples in the world today. The second lecture we will consider the specific worldviews we will discuss in this lecture series.

Worldview Characteristics

Several characteristics of worldview should be mentioned and described in any discussion about worldviews.

First, worldview is learned (absorbed) from the environment in which a person lives. As part of the process of enculturation,[14] the baby begins to learn not only the language and customs but also the suppositions, premises, and concepts from their parents, family, and surrounding community. It is, therefore, expected that a child born in a Muslim environment will grow with a Muslim worldview and a child born to parents who have an Animist worldview will identify with this worldview.

Second, a worldview is learned (or absorbed) before the person has the ability to analyze and evaluate it. For example, in a culture with an animistic worldview if a baby is getting close to a piece of bread on the ground, the mother says, "Do not eat the bread because it has evil spirits and they will make you sick." In a home of people with a scientific worldview, however, the mother tells the child: "Do not put that piece of bread in your mouth because it has germs and you will get sick."

In both cases, the children accept the explanation of their mother and do not question it because they do not have the capacity for such thinking at an early age. It is inconceivable that the child would ask the mother: "Do you subscribe to the germ theory to explain the disease?" The truth is that most of the time people receive and retain a worldview without questioning it. The suppositions of worldviews are not reasoned, but assumed. For this reason a vast diversity in worldviews exists around the world.

Third, the premises and suppositions of a worldview generally are in the subconscious areas of peoples' thinking unless something happens that causes people to be aware of them.[15] Levi De Carvalho explains:

> Part of the cultural behavior of man is conscious, for example, the language he uses, the relationship with his group, the common practices, parties, ceremonies and so on. But there is another part that is usually subconscious-for example, the values that one has, the way of understanding the universe, the beliefs that a person has and becomes aware of them only when he meets people who have a different perspective of life.[16]

Paul Hiebert affirms this idea when he says: "Worldviews are mostly implicit. As the lenses we use, it is difficult for us to see our worldview."[17] This truth has important implications to be discussed in more detail later. Suffice it to say here that it is possible that we ourselves are not aware of the premises and suppositions of our worldviews as we are involved in evangelistic work in trans-cultural contexts. One objective of these conferences is to arrive at a clearer understanding of our worldview which will enable us to understand the worldviews of peoples from other cultures. It is also important to mention that usually people from other cultures are also not aware of the premises and suppositions of their worldviews.

For this reason in most cases it is not enough to ask them to tell us what the premises and suppositions of their worldviews are. The process of identifying the worldview of another cultural group is difficult and complicated. This act requires more than an academic study. The method that the discipline of Anthropology uses, "observation and participation," provides the best opportunity to identify and understand the worldview of another cultural group. Using this method, anthropologists live among the cultural group, observe their practices, participate in its activities (as far as they can), and ask questions to clarify their observations.

Fourth, a distinction exists between worldview and religion. In his book, *Worldview: Crosscultural Explorations of Human Beliefs*, Ninian Smart defines worldviews in terms of "ideologies, both religious and secular of a people group."[18] Worldview and religion are not exactly the same but are closely related.

Although worldview and religion have aspects that are intertwined, there are significant differences that must be understood. Worldview consists of the core suppositions and concepts concerning life on which people base their behavior. Religion is the part of these suppositions that deal with supernatural beings and rites, ceremonies, and ethical circumstances of these beliefs. Religion is more than worldview because it includes not only beliefs but practices and behavior of individuals. Worldview encompasses a large number of beliefs related to the supernatural. Worldview provides the basis for all subsystems in addition to religion. In this sense, worldview is potentially more than the religious belief system. We must, however, make one exception. In animistic cultures, worldview and religion are almost synonymous. Since in these cultures people believe that all that happens is attributed to the spiritual forces and is interpreted from a supernatural perspective, it is almost impossible to distinguish between worldview and religion. In this case the terms are interchangeable.

Fifth, worldview is at the center of all the subsystems of a culture. This includes the technological, social, political, linguistic, economic, and religious subsystems. The way the subsystems are established and operated reflects the cultural group's worldview. For example, in an animistic system, spirits are consulted for all decisions and activities. Among other things, this practice has two important implications for cross-cultural workers. First, the cross cultural worker cannot know a sociocultural group until he/she understands their worldview. Second, a change in any subsystem produces changes through the culture and in all subsystems of a sociocultural group.

Functions of Worldview

Worldview functions in several ways and we must take these into account in our cultural ministry. N. T. Wright points out several important functions worldview provides in every culture. He explains:

> In the cognitive level worldview gives us a rational justification for our beliefs and integrates them into a perspective of reality more or less unified. At the level of values, worldview gives validation to our deeper cultural norms."[19]

In this section we will briefly discuss the main functions of a worldview.

The first function of worldview is to *explain*. Worldview explains how things came to be that way and what keeps them that way. If it is a naturalistic worldview, it explains that the universe is controlled by man. If it is an animistic worldview, it explains that the universe is controlled by spirits. These worldviews are articulated in the mythology of the people which may include folklore, science, or history.

The second function of worldview is to *validate*. This means that worldview gives its approval to the basic institutions, values, and goals of society. This feature gives people the impression that their approach to life is real and correct. For example, worldviews of democratic societies affirm the values of private enterprise, the scientific method, rights and liberties, private property, and public education. Likewise, the worldviews of autocratic societies sanction very different values related to governmental, social and economic systems.

The third function of worldview is to *provide psychological reinforcement*. This provision includes support in times of crisis and vulnerability. Support includes such experiences as the death of a loved one, birth of a child, times of illness, and transitions such as marriage, puberty, time of sowing, harvest time, and periods of uncertainty caused by personal, regional, or national crises. The rites and ceremonies are often important mechanisms of support. Depending on their worldview, this may include prayer, scientific experimentation, visiting a counselor, offering sacrifices, consulting a healer, or trying to communicate with the spirits of their ancestors.

The fourth function of worldview is *integration*. Worldview organizes and systematizes the perceptions of reality into an overall design. According to their worldview, people conceptualize what they should be like and they interpret their experiences according to this conceptualization. Worldview provides a bridge between the perceptions of reality outside the people's heads and inside their heads according to predetermined patterns.

The fifth function of worldview is *adaptation*. This includes adjusting the model to a new perception of reality. It also involves reinterpreting earlier perceptions to conform to new perceptions. This process can happen on a global scale. For example, Western society has gone through the stages of the Middle Age, the Renaissance, the Industrial Revolution, the Scientific Age, and today is struggling with Post Modernism. This has changed the society of absolute dependence on the Judeo/Christian God to man's belief in human ability and technology.

Christian workers of necessity must seek to understand the functions of worldview in order that these workers might stimulate changes in the worldviews of the people to whom they minister. Effective change of a culture depends on a change in their worldview. The Bible teaches that "if the root of the tree is dedicated to God, so are the branches" (Rom 11:16).

Importance of Worldview

One of the questions asked frequently is, why should we take the time to identify the worldview of a cultural group? Some people believe that we should just preach to the people of other cultures without having to worry about their worldview. These workers do not seem to be aware of the possibility that people may listen but not understand or misunderstand the gospel message because it has not been presented in a manner that takes their worldview into account. Others believe that basic information (demographic and sociological) on the culture of the people is enough without taking time away from the task of evangelization. Still other workers consider the task of knowing the worldview as an activity of academic interest with no practical implications.

It is instructive to note that when the people at Lystra saw the miracle of healing involved in the ministry of Paul, they interpreted in the light of their worldview. They said, *"Gods in the likeness of men have come down to us."* And they called Barnabas Jupiter and Paul Mercury, because he was speaking the word (Acts 14:11-12).

Seeing this demonstration, Paul and Barnabas did their best to present the biblical worldview (vv. 14-17). Even so, this story ends: *"And with these saying they could scarcely refrain the crowd from sacrificing to them"* (v.18). Cultural workers should be aware that listeners usually interpret the message through the filter of their own worldviews.

Understanding worldview is essential to communicating the gospel. Contributors to the Willowbank Report, in connection with the Lausanne movement, emphasized the need to understand the culture and worldview of cultural groups. They wrote:

> At its center is a worldview, that is, a general understanding of the nature of universe and one's place in it. This may be "religious" (about God of gods and spirits, and our relation to them), or it man express a "secular"

concept of reality, as in a Marxist society. From this basic worldview flow both standards of judgment or values (of which is good in the sense of desirable, of what is acceptable in accordance with the general will of the community and of the countries) and the standard of conduct ...

No Christian witness can hope to communicate the gospel if he or she ignores the cultural factor. This is particularly true in the case of missionaries. For they are themselves the product of one and go to people who are the product of another culture ... The other problem is that the gospel is often presented to people in alien culture forms... Sensitive cross-cultural missionaries will not arrive at their sphere of service with a pre-packaged gospel. They must have a clear grasp of the "given" truth of the gospel. But they will fail to communicate successfully if they try to impose this on people without reference to their cultural situation and that of the people to whom they go. It is only by active loving engagement with the local people, thinking in their thought patterns, understanding their worldview, listening to their questions, and feeling their burdens, that the whole believing community (of which the missionary is a part) will be able to respond to the need.[20]

James Slack, missionary worker with the International Mission Board, affirms the importance of understanding worldview to communicate the gospel effectively. He says: "The basic reason for identifying a person's worldview is to share the story of Christ in such a way that it makes sense to them."[21] Worldview analysis can give us an idea of the biblical teachings people need to know to make an informed decision to receive Christ as their personal Savior. Such analysis can also help you find some bridges of communication. Are there any cultural stories, beliefs or concepts in their worldviews that can serve as redemptive analogies or bridges to communicate the gospel?

A second reason why we must know the worldview of a sociocultural group is that it can help us identify barriers to the gospel that exist within that group. What are the beliefs and practices that hinder a group of people in understanding and accepting the message of salvation? Some of the barriers may be ignorance, apathy, cultural traditions, beliefs and unbiblical practices, fear of disrupting the harmony of the community, or fear of disturbing the spirit world. The study of worldviews may reveal what the barriers are and provide information to help you know how to overcome them.

The third reason why you must identify the local group's worldview is that if this is not done, the cultural workers will tend to present the gospel message from their own perspective. Slack explains that "when the missionary presents the gospel with his own cultural wrapping, there will be a transplantation of concepts related to church polity and lifestyles of the believers that will not fit in the new environment."[22]

Although there are other reasons why workers should study the worldview of cultural groups, the last we will mention is that such cross-cultural study will help the worker recognize that in reality he or she is working in the context of various worldviews. As Slack says, "there is the worldview of the un-evangelized group, the worldview of cultural workers, the worldview of the Bible where the message originates, and the worldview of the group of local churches. Studies indicate that those who have no sensitivity to worldviews and have not compared their own worldview with that of the Bible are programmed to reproduce their worldview in any environment in which they work.[23]

In this lecture we have attempted to define the term "worldview." Then we focused our attention on worldview characteristics, its main functions, and its importance in cross-cultural work. In the following discussion we will give our attention to the specific characteristics of the animistic worldview.

Reflection

1. Identify the worldview or worldviews in which you grew up

    a. Main premises (you can use the questions in James Sire at the end of each section) Practices influenced by the worldview

    b. Conflicts between the worldviews if you grew up in more than one

2. Describe how you were influenced by this worldview in the way you think and act

3. If you have experienced a change in your worldview as a result of your conversion to the gospel, describe this change

    a. Did the people who presented the gospel message to you show sensitivity to your worldview?

    b. How did they deal with the bridges and barriers in your worldview?

    c. Did the people that evangelized you take into account your worldview in the discipleship method they utilized?

4. If you have done evangelistic work with people from another worldview, describe that worldview and how you have adapted the presentation of the gospel in that context

5. How do you answer a person who thinks it's a waste of time to study the worldview of a sociocultural group but believes that the only important thing is to "preach the gospel"?

6. Write any question(s) that you still have with regard to the concept of worldview

7. Compare the way the Apostle Paul took into account the worldviews when he communicated the message of salvation to Jews (Acts 13:13-39) and to the Gentiles in Athens (Acts 17:16-34)

James Sire suggests seven questions to express worldview in prepositions:

1. What is prime reality—what is really real?

2. What is the nature of external reality, i.e., the world around us?
3. What is a human being?
4. What happens when a person dies?
5. Why is it possible to know something?
6. How do we know what is good and what is bad?
7. What is the meaning of human history?

Assignment: Ask yourself these questions, write answers, evaluate and describe their worldview

Bibliography

Andrew Atkins. "Know Your Own Culture: A Neglected Tool for Cross-Cultural Ministry" *EMQ* 26 (July *1990): 266 -71.*

Bowen, Earle and Dorothy Bowen. "Contextualizing Teaching Methods in Africa" *EMQ* 25 (July 1989): 270 -5.

Burnett, *David. Clash of Worlds.* Nashville: Oliver Nelson, Thomas Nelson, 1992.

Congdon, Garth D. "An Investigation into the Current Zulu and Its Relevance to Missionary Work." *CME* 21 (July 1985).

Depew, Michael. "Paul and the Contextualization of the Gospel." http://pages.preferred.com/ ~ mdepew/mis1.html

Elmer, Duane. *Cross-Cultural Connections: Stepping Out & Fitting In Around the World.* Downers Grove, IL: InterVarsity Press, 2002.

Grady, Dick, and Glenn Kendall. "Seven Keys to Effective Church Planting." *EMQ* 28 (October 1992): 366 -73.

Hesselgrave, David J. "Contextualization That Is Authentic and Relevant." *International Journal of Frontier Missions* 12, no. 3 (July-Sept. 1995): 115 -9.

_____. "Great Commission Contextualization." *International Journal of Frontier Missions 12,* no. *3* (July-Sept. 1995): 139-44.

Hiebert, Paul. "Critical Contextualization." *Missiology: An International Review* 12, no. 3 (July 1984): 287 -96.

_____. "Critical Contextualization." *International Bulletin of Missionary Research* 11 (July 1987): 104 -12.

_____. "The Flaw of the Excluded Middle." *Missiology: An International Review* 10, no. 1 (January 1982): 35 -47.

Jacobs, Donald R. "Culture and Phenomena of Conversions: Reflections in an East Africa Setting." *Gospel in Context (July 1978):* 4-14.

Jenkins, Orville Boyd. *Dealing with Differences: Contrasting African and European Worldviews.* Nairobi: Communication Press, 1991.

Kraft, Charles H. *Christianity with Power: You and Your Experience of the Supernatural.* Ann Arbor, MI: Vine, Servant, 1989.

May, Stanley O. "Short Term Mission Trips are Great If. . . "*CME* 36, no. 4 (October 2000): 444-9.

_____. "Cultures and Worldviews," in *Discovering the Mission of God,* ed. Mike Barnett and Robin Martin. Downers Grove, IL: IVP Academic, 2012.

Muller, Roland. *Honor and Shame: Unlocking the Door.* Np: Xlibris, 2000.

_____. *Tools for Muslim Evangelism.* Belleville, Ontario, Canada: Essence Publishing, 2000. see also www.rmuller.com

Moreau, Scott. "The Human Universals of Culture: Implications for Contextualization." *International Journal of Frontier Missions* 12, no. 3 (July-Sept. 1995): 121 -5.

Parshall, Phil. "Danger! New Directions in Contextualization." *CME* 34 (October 1998): 404 -10.

Racey, David. "Contextualization: How Far Is Too Far?" *EMQ* 32 (July 1996): 304 -10.

Sawatsky, Ben. "What It Takes to Be a Church Planter." *CME* 27 (October 1991): 342 -7.

Sire, James W. *How to Read Slowly: Reading for Comprehension.* Wheaton: Harold Shaw Publishers, 1978.

Thomas, Bruce. "The Gospel for Shame Cultures," *CME* 30 (July 1994): 284 -90.

Winter, Ralph D. "Christian History in Cross-Cultural Perspective" *International Journal of Frontier Missions* 12, no. 3 (July-Sept. 1995): 127-32

CHAPTER 2

Animistic Worldview

In the first session we focused on the concept or meaning of worldview. In this session we will turn our attention to the Animistic Worldview.

Many of the world's religions are based on an animistic worldview. In fact, animism is so common and widespread that many authorities consider it the basis for nearly fifty percent of all world religions. Gailyn Van Rheenen notes that,

> Stephen C. Neill has estimated that 40 percent of the world's populations base their lives on animistic thinking. Because animism frequently hides behind the facade of other world religions, Neill's already high percentage is probably a low estimate.[24]

If Neill's statement is accurate, animism rules the lives of more people than any other religion in the world. Many animists currently reside in the Pacific Islands, in South Asia, Australia, India, Siberia, and North and South America.[25] Clearly, the study of animism and its impact on the lives of people on this continent holds great significance.

Before describing the main features of animism I will make several observations. First, there is not just one animistic worldview. A variety of animistic worldviews exists and thrives throughout the world. For this reason, we will try to present a generic animistic worldview. Although great diversity exists among the worldviews of animistic peoples, significant unanimity on the premises and basic suppositions of these worldviews in different parts of the world make a generic approach feasible.

Second, some people do not like the term "animism." They think this is a derogatory term that shows a spirit of cultural superiority. In view of this feeling, some prefer the term "tribal religions" or "primitive religions," or "traditional religions." The truth is that as Alan R. Tippett observed, all of these terms have their weaknesses because animism is very active not only in tribal cultures but also in large urban areas like Los Angeles, New Orleans, or San Pablo and it is not chronologically or conceptually primitive.[26]

In this presentation, therefore we use the term "animism," not with any suggestion of disrespect but only because it has been used officially by the social sciences and because much of the academic literature and religious uses it. We understand and respect, however, the decision of some people to use another term to describe this worldview.

Definition of the term "Animism"

Edward B. Tylor (1832-1917), recognized as the founder of modern anthropology, established the use of the term "animism" to mean "belief in spiritual beings."[27] He explains:

> Animism in its full development includes the belief in souls and in a future existence, in

> controlling deities and subordinate spirits...
> resulting in some kind of active worship.[28]

> These spirits include both those of living ancestors
> "capable of continued existence after death" and
> other spirits, rising to the rank of powerful
> deities."[29]

Pablo Deiros defines animism as, "The belief that the world in which I live is controlled by personal and impersonal spirits, that some of those spirits affect me, and that it is important for me to identify which are the spirits that affect me and to search for options to please them and to gain some degree of success in life."[30] Gailyn Van Rheenen defines animism as "the belief that spiritual beings and impersonal spiritual forces have power over human affairs and, consequently, that human beings discover what beings and forces are influencing them in order to determine future action and frequently to manipulate their powers."[31]

Eugene A. Nida defines animism as "the belief in spirits, including spirits of dead people as much as those without human origin."[32] Howard Douglas defines the term in a way that describes some of their practices:

> Animism is the belief in many spiritual beings
> and souls that inhabit the universe, whose
> existence is found in people or in nature. Usually
> these are conceptualized as autonomous beings
> representing different spheres of influence over
> nature (such as trees, water, animals, weather,
> etc..) or places (such as mountains, deserts,
> forests, etc..) or human beings (disease-causing,

inducing behavior of possession, evil behavior, or helping, etc.).[33]

In all these definitions it is clear that animism is the belief in spiritual beings (dead persons, deities, and impersonal forces) that influence all aspects of the life of human beings and should be indulged, placated or controlled.

With this as a basic definition now we describe the suppositions of the animistic worldview.

Animistic Suppositions

Animistic worldview is based on a number of suppositions. Due to limitations of time and space we will focus only on the main suppositions of this worldview. These suppositions include:

- all nature is interconnected,
- the universe is filled spirits and powers,
- these powers can be controlled,
- and divination is essential.

All Nature is Interconnected

The animistic worldview sees a unity in all nature. Van Rheenen explains this supposition when he says:

> Animists believe that all of life is interconnected. People are intimately linked, some of them are living and some of whom have already passed into the spiritual realm. They are connected to the spiritual world ... Animists feel connectedness with nature. The stars, planets and the moon are thought to affect earthly events. The natural realm is so related to the human realm that practitioners divine current and future events by

24

analyzing what the animals are doing or by sacrificing animals and analyzing their livers, entrails, or stomachs. Many animists believe they are connected with other human beings.[34]

Because of this supposed unity the animistic worldview does not distinguish between humans and animals. Animals may be ancestors of the people. People can turn into animals, trees, or rocks which may possess souls.[35] Eugene Nida says:

In fact, in some groups, almost every object in the universe is viewed as possessing some amount of life force - the spiritual, non-material substance, without which nothing could exist and that in reality is the true character and the secret of its power ... Almost as important as spatial identification with the nature around him, or temporal association with the ancestors and descendants, is the animist's understanding of himself as psychologically akin to the inhabitants of the spirit world.[36]

The writers of Lausanne Report further state that the people who live under an animistic worldview consider themselves to be connected with the universe. They explain:

People see themselves as living in relationship to other persons, to their physical environment and to the spiritual world. Because they have a strong corporate sense and personal experience deep relationships with other persons in social groups, personal decisions are frequently made in terms of these groups.[37]

As you can see in these statements, the lives of people with an animistic worldview are interconnected with the physical world, the spiritual world, the spirits of living beings, and of the dead. As a result of this supposition, the lives of people are intertwined with nature and the spiritual world. Since they do not separate these two worlds, as people with a Western worldviews characteristically do, everything that happens in their life is related to the spirits. The practice of ancestor worship, for example, has not only family implications but also social and spiritual. The belief that the souls of loved ones come back in the lives of those who are born in that community reflects this concept of interconnectedness in animistic worldviews.

An African student in our seminary, who suffered the loss of his elderly mother due to illness, still has to fight to reject the idea in his mind that his daughter who was born recently has the soul of his mother. One thing that makes it difficult to reject this idea, apart from the fact that he grew up with this tradition even in a Christian home, is that his daughter resembles her grandmother.

The Universe Is Filled With Spirits and Powers

The animistic worldview begins with the supposition that the universe is filled with spirits of the gods, ancestors, the spirits (ghosts), and a wide variety of other kinds of spirits. These various spirits and other entities such as material objects have power, or the capacity to affect life and history.

The writers of Lausanne Report on Traditional Religions explained:

Some are aloof. Others are active in the everyday lives of people intervening, helping, hindering and influencing events in their lives. Some are good, some are evil, but most tend to be capricious. It is important to emphasize that, for most practitioners of traditional religions, elements of that spirit world are present and active in this world. Although they may be unseen, there *are not* unknown or removed from the everyday affairs of people.[38]

Gailyn Van Rheenen expresses this supposition in a similar way when he says:

The animists assume that the visible world is related to the unseen world. An interaction exists between the divine and the human, the sacred and the profane, the holy and the secular. The influences of God, gods, spirits and ancestors affect the living. Humans are thought to be controlled by spiritual forces, whether they are ancestors or ghosts, gods or spirits, witchcraft or sorcery and curses or the evil eye. They in turn seek to appease the powers through sacrifices and libations to access power to cope with evil through ritual, and to protect themselves through charms and amulets.[39]

Nida adds that Animists believe that spirits affect all areas of their lives. He explains:

From conception to death, from morning till night, from spring until harvest, and from the start of any enterprise (like building a house or hunting hippos) until its end, supernatural forces are present and must be properly dealt with or failure is inevitable.[40]

This belief in the spirit world controls all activities of animists. Many of the animistic religious practices are motivated by fear of offending the spirits or of ignoring the rites and ceremonies that can result in both personal and communal punishment. Their lives are often oppressed by terror-related situations, places, actions (such as evil eye) that can cause illness or even death. In short, the world is full of animistic spirits, some good, some bad, but all with the power to affect their lives. Those who live with the animistic worldview live in constant fear of powers outside their control.

Powers Can Be Controlled

Animistic thinking conceives the powers as being subject to control. The world of the person who follows the animistic worldview is full of powers that can be used for good or for bad depending on how people relate to them. Nida explains:

> One basic supposition that is implied in all animistic practices is that the controllability of the spirit power. If one only knows the right formula, the spirit world can be made to do one's bidding whether for good or for evil. The animist is not concerned about seeking the will of his god, but in compelling, entreating, or coercing his god to do his will.[41]

Van Rheenen adds:

> An animist's relationship with spiritual beings is viewed in terms of power. Spiritual beings are propitiated, coerced, or placated because they have power. The magic ritual is employed because of its power to influence impersonal forces and spiritual beings... Various methodologies of divination are employed to determine what power is causing misfortune or illness or what powers must be employed to counter such negative power. Animism is a

religion of power based upon manipulation and coercion of spiritual powers.[42]

Philip Steyne asserts that,

> This power can be obtained by manipulating a ritual which may take the form of sacrifices, offerings, taboos, fetishes, ceremonies, and even witchcraft and sorcery. Power can also be obtained by the laying on of hands or finding a spiritual, religious status or using clothing or something that was previously associated with that person. It must be obtained whatever the cost.[43]

These powers can be personal or impersonal. Personal forces of the animistic worldview can be a hierarchy of spiritual beings. These may include the most-high God creator of the universe who is not involved and is separated. Below this High God there is a multitude of lesser gods and spirits which people must please.

In addition to the personal spirit there are impersonal spirits. These may include chiefs of the spirits of the earth, sky, sea, animals, and fire. There are also evil spirits (demons) that can take possession of people. You can also add to these mischievous spirits who scare people if not treated with respect.

The Animistic Worldview also conceives of inanimate objects that have spiritual power. Anthropologists often use the Polynesian term "mana" to describe this type of power. A particular object such as an unusual rock, a boat, an oar, or some other object may be thought to have special power and be used by those who follow Animistic Worldview.

Divination is Essential

The animistic worldview assumes and teaches that practitioners (Shamans, Healers, Warlocks, Priests, etc.) can discover the causes of diseases, curses, setbacks, and predict the future of the people. The practice of divination is based on the supposition that you can communicate with the spirits and get the information you want. Van Rheenen describes the practice of divination in the following way:

> Diviners use innumerable and varied types of methods to determine the will of spiritual powers. They check omens, use astrology, divine by technique, employ ordeals, rely on guidance from the dead, interpret dreams and visions and divine while possessed. These types of divination based on the conception that the universe functions harmoniously as an organism. The stars of the heavens, the signs of nature, the dreams of the night and wisher of spiritual beings are interrelated and connected to the events which occur in the world. What happens in one part of the organism is reflected in its other parts. Astrologist reads the signs of the heavens to determine the workings of the world. He believes that these elements work harmoniously in an interconnected world.[44]

Followers of Animistic Worldviews hold to other suppositions in addition to these we have considered. Due to limitations of space and time we will, however, limit ourselves to those we have already presented because these suppositions are the most basic and most widely held.[45]

Animism and the Scriptures

Cultural workers facing animist practices are not without resources to respond effectively. The first and most authoritative resource is the Word of God. Without going into extensive detail we can show examples of how the Bible deals with animism in a direct or indirect manner.

Animism in the Old Testament

The book of Leviticus provides clear instructions on the proper worship of God and the types of offerings that are acceptable. In 1 Samuel chapter 28 we find the judgment of God against Saul for consulting the witch of Endor. In 1 Kings 18 we find the description of the power encounter that Elijah had with the prophets of Baal. In this event, four realities are evident:

1) The question (Who is the true God? v. 21),
2) The ordeal (The one that sends fire is the true God. v. 22-24),
3) The climax (Lord sent fire and consumed the burnt offering. v. 39) and
4) The verdict ("The Lord, is God." v. 39).

In Isaiah 57 the God condemns animistic practices through the Prophet. The Israelites are called *"sons of the sorceress"* (v. 3). They are accused of worshiping trees (v.5), of sacrificing their children (v. 5), of offering libations (v. 6), and using fetishes (v. 8). After these charges, God reveals his nature as Lord of the universe (vv. 14-21).

31

The Old Testament records some evidences of animistic type practices among God's people but consistently reveals the error of such efforts. God must be worshiped and served in spiritual ways not by magic means.

Power Encounters In the New Testament

In the New Testament we read of the power encounters that emphasize the superior power of God. In Mark 1:21-28 Jesus commands the demon to be silent. In Luke 8:26-39 Jesus frees the Gadarene demoniac from demonic bondage. In Samaria, Philip works miracles of deliverance (Acts 8:7-24). In Philippi Paul frees the slave girl who earned money by divination (Acts 16:17-27). In 1 Corinthians 10:20-21 Paul warns the believers against the animist practice of sacrificing to demons. In Ephesians 6:12 Paul clearly teaches that *"we wrestle not against flesh and blood but against principalities, against powers, against the rulers of the darkness of this world, against spiritual wickedness in high places."*

In short, the Bible, the most authoritative book on animistic practices, clearly disclaims and prohibits the practice of seeking power and advance by calling on spiritual beings or powers. Animistic practices are not in line with biblical teachings.

The Christian Response
to Animism

The Christian message has a solid and powerful response to those who are enslaved to animistic practices. Freedom from spiritual bondage is available to all through the power of the God of the Bible. To be effective, Christian workers must be prepared as cultural workers and then have an effective strategy to use in the struggle with the spiritual forces.

Preparation of the Workers

In his article "The Flaw Of The Excluded Middle," Paul G. Hiebert stresses the fact that the worldview of the Western culture has eliminated the level of supernatural beings and forces in this world.[46] He explains that the Western perspective has only two levels of reality. One level, the religious, includes faith, miracles, problems of the other world (spiritual), and explains that which is sacred. The second level, the scientific, includes sight, experience, the natural order, the problems of this world and that which is secular.

Hiebert explains that going to the mission field he was not prepared to face the challenges of the middle level which included the animistic practices of individuals and the presence of evil spirits in the lives of people. He says: "I was used to presenting Christ with rational arguments, not with evidence of his power in the lives of people who were sick, possessed and destitute." He further explains: "As a scientist I was trained to deal with the empirical world in naturalistic

33

terms. As a theologian I was taught how to answer the ultimate questions in theistic terms. For me there was no middle area."[47] We do not have the time or space to address this issue in more detail. What we can do is emphasize that in the preparation of cultural workers it is absolutely necessary to pay attention to the "excluded middle."

Areas of study

Certain necessities should be central in the preparation of workers who will serve people who follow an Animistic Worldview. The intercultural worker should be knowledgeable about the beliefs and practices of animists. These necessities include:

- Study and observation with regard to magic (practice of manipulation of spirits and powers);

- Medicine men (practice of seeking healing from the spirits);

- Witchcraft (the utilization of black magic to cast spells and cause harm);

- Ancestor Worship (seeking to communicate with their spirits);

- Purification rituals (to obtain cleansing and power);

- Divination (seeking information and direction from the spirits), demonic possession (persons controlled by demons);

- Spiritual Warfare (confrontations with the evil spirits);

- Functional substitutes (practices that are biblically solid and culturally relevant to fill the voids in the lives of people who have abandoned animism).

Other beliefs and practices within Animism demand to be studied. Those mentioned here are the most basic and commonly observed in animistic cultures. The study of the animistic worldview can help workers identify cultural barriers as well bridges to communicate the gospel.

Recommendation of Strategies

In his article entitled "The Evangelization of Animists" Dr. Alan R. Tippett gives practical suggestions to one who is seeking to guide the animists to a personal and exclusive faith in Jesus Christ. As a preface he explains the situations that face missionaries:

- Pay attention to the conversion of animists and their incorporation into fellowship groups. This involves us in each one of the following problems that I have conceptualized anthropologically and I believe that this approach opens up for us the best theme for our discussion.[48]

- Pay attention to the problem of encounter. Animists do just drift to the Christian faith... Even if it is true that there are sympathizers that come under the influence of the Spirit of God, the transition from paganism to the Christian faith is a clear and definite act, a specific change in a person's life, a "coming out of to a going into" something very different, a change of loyalty or in the biblical analogy, a change of citizenship (Eph 2:12-13). The book of Joshua (24:15) ends with the specific scene: Choose you this day whom you will serve...

- Pay attention to the problem of motivation. The Animist may be interested in Christianity for a variety reasons–some good, others bad. When people say they want to receive Christ, do they wish to add him to their collection of gods or spirits? Do they want to gain power as Simon did? (Acts 8:9-24).

I do not want to give the impression that all animists are like that. There are thousands who sincerely receive Christ. But we must ask the question - What is the role of the pastoral counselor when a prospective convert is about to respond to the gospel?

- Pay attention to the problem of meaning of the expressions they use. The words may be similar but the meaning may be very different. Such terms as (e.g., sacrifice, salvation, liberation, and purification, etc.) have a theological meaning for us, but are used in very different ways in animistic contexts.

- Pay attention to social structures. What are the implications for the lifestyle of new converts? People to whom the evangelist goes may organize their lives in a very different from his and he should remember that the process of evangelization should guide him in the formation of fellowship groups and these should have autonomous structures and not foreign ones.

- Pay attention to the problem of incorporation. One of the challenges of biblical evangelism is that of making provision for incorporating the converts into a fellowship. The Great Commission does not end with making disciples but continues saying "baptizing and teaching them" (Matt 18: 19, 20).

- Pay attention to the problem of the voids in the lives of the new converts. This applies to the celebrations of the rites of passage (e.g., births, weddings, funerals, etc...). If these voids are not filled with functional substitutes, believers will continue to practice them in syncretistic ways.

- Pay attention to cultural voids. A basic question surfaces: What does it means to be a convert from the animistic world and participate in a fellowship of converted animists? How does the convert from animism meet his physical and spiritual needs that emerge from his previous lifestyle - problems of danger, death, disease or witchcraft - how does he discover God's will for his life?[49]

Van Rheenen adds these words of instruction:

The role of the Christian minister is to direct the attention of the animistic to the cross - the symbol of the great sacrifice of the Son of God to cleanse from sin and liberate from Satan. The great message to the animist is that God entered human history powerfully through the ministry and death of

Christo break the chains of Satan. Christ has "disarmed the powers and authorities" (Col 2:15). So for the Christian in an animistic society, the cross means *liberation*-liberation from demonic forces against which he is fighting, release of the rules and requirements that these powers are trying to impose on society, and freedom from sin that has separated the people of God and has caused the lack of harmony in society. . . He must proclaim the sovereignty of God in word and in deed. . . In proclaiming the sovereignty of God and humanity's total loyalty to him, the principalities and powers are being defeated. ("Defining an Animistic Worldview," 2003).

In conclusion we can say that a detailed study of the suppositions, beliefs and practices of the animistic worldview can help develop contextualized evangelism and discipleship strategies in these contexts. This study may begin with a discussion of the suppositions of the animistic worldview. A summary of the animistic worldview must include the following suppositions:

- There is a supreme God but He is distant;

- The animist struggles against the spirits, that although they are inferior to God, he feels he must fear and pacify them with offerings and sacrifices:

- All diseases are caused by evil spirits, so therefore, they need a Shaman to discover where these diseases come from;

- There is life after death and sacrifices should be offered to the spirits of those who have died so they will cause good instead of harm.

- Everything in the universe and the world is interconnected;

- Power is needed to control the world the spirits.

All these suppositions should be evaluated in light of biblical teachings. Then the worker must make an intercultural analysis of his own worldview and how it will help or a hinder his ministry in animistic cultures. As a result, the development of strategies to reach these groups with the gospel message will be informed by the knowledge acquired.

Reflection

1. How much do we know about our own worldview? Is there a mixture of worldviews in our minds?

2. To what extend has our worldview prepared us to know how to minister in animistic cultures? Is our worldview a help or a hindrance?

3. How effective have the denominations with which we work been in helping us in dealing with the animistic worldview?

4. How contextualized have the evangelization, discipleship and leadership training strategies been in animistic cultures?

5. Do a study of Simon the sorcerer in Acts 8. Answer the following questions: 1. What was his occupation before the arrival of Philip? (vv. 9-11); 2. Did Simon believe Phillip's message? (vv. 11-13); 3. Was Simon baptized?

(v. 13); 4. What did Simon ask of Peter? (vv. 14-19); 5. What was Peter's response? (v. 20-22); 6. According to Peter was Simon truly converted? (vv. 20-23); 7. Did Simon repent or was he simply trying to avoid punishment? (v. 24); 8. What can we learn about the motivation and some animists?

6. Eugene Nida describes the weaknesses of the animistic beliefs as follows:

- There is no fundamental moral basis in animism;

- Animism provides no satisfactory answers to the question of the meaning of life and the significance of history;

- Often the religious leaders--shamans, sorcerers, mediums – are on the "lunatic fringe" of society. They are often psychotic, mentally deranged, emotionally unstable;

- The undue emphasis upon the psychological and infantile religious practices...sacrifices, the preservation of skulls, fertility orgies, ritual prostitution, etc ... The primitive religions directly or indirectly encourage many antisocial practices, fear of witches, suspicion of black magic, loss of life through initiation ceremonies, head hunting, the erratic divination for making social decisions, and dependence on emotionally unstable people who dominate not only the religious activities of that group but also the political and economic areas of lives as well.[50]

Questions:

1. How many of the weaknesses that Nida has mentioned have you observed in animistic cultures?

2. What answer can you give from the Bible to the weaknesses mentioned by Nida?

3. How can the weaknesses be used as bridges to communicate gospel in animistic settings?

Bibliography

Adeyemo, Tokunboh. *Salvation in African Tradition*. Nairobi: Evangel Publishing House, 1979.

Blakeslee, Virginia, *Religion in a Changing, World*, 21-38. Chicago: Moody Press, 1959.

Brown, Colin, ed., Sacrifice, first fruits, altar, offering. *In The New International Dictionary of New Testament Theology*. Grand Rapids: Zondervan, 1988.

Burnett, David, *Unearthly Powers*. Eastbourne, England: MARC, 1988.

Burnett, Bryant L. Myers, General Editor, *Evangelical Dictionary of World Missions*. Grand Rapids: Baker Book House, 2000.

Arnold, Clinton E. *Ephesians: Power and Magic. Society for New Testament* Studies, Monograph Series. New York: Cambridge University Press, 1989.

Deiros, Pablo Alberto. *Diccionario Hispano-Americano De La Misión.* 1997.

Dickson, Kwesi and Paul Ellingworth, eds., *Biblical Revelation and African Beliefs*. London: Lutterworth Press, 1969.

Hesselgrave, David J. , *Communicating Christ Cross-Culturally.* Grand Rapids: Zondervan, 1978.

Hiebert, Paul. 1978. *Phenomenology and institutions of Animism*. Syllabus for B620. Pasadena: Fuller Theological Seminary.

Hiebert, Paul G, "The flaw of the excluded middle," *Missiology.* Vol. X, No. 1 (January 1982): 35-47

Shaw, R. Daniel & Tienou, Tite . *Understanding Folk Religion: A Christian Response to Popular Beliefs and Practices.* Grand Rapids: Baker Books, 1999.

Kipkorir, B.E,. *The Marakwet of Kenya* . Nairobi, Kenya: East African Literature Bureau, 1973.

Kraft, Charles. *Christianity in Culture.* New York: Orbis Books, 1980

Kraft, Charles H. "Contextualization and spiritual power." In *Deliver Us From Evil: An Uneasy Frontier in Christian Mission,* eds. A Scott Moreau, Tokunboh Adeyemo, David G. Burnett, Bryant L. Myers and Hwa Yung. Monrovia, CA: MARC: World Vision International, 2000.

_____. "Power Encounter." In *Evangelical Dictionary of World Missions* , ed. A Scott Moreau. *Grand Rapids: Baker Book House,* 2000.

Leach, Edmund. *Culture and Communication* . Cambridge: Cambridge University Press, 1976.

Mbiti, John S. *African Religions and Philosophy* . London: Heinemann, 1969.

_____. "God, sin and salvation in African religion." AME *Zion Quarterly Review* 100 (1989): 2-8.

McClintock, Wayne, "Demons and Ghosts in Indian Folklore. " *Missiology* 18 (Jan.): 37-48, 1990.

Moreau, A. Scott. General Editor, *Deliver Us from Evil: An Uneasy Frontier in Christian Mission*. Monrovia, California: World Vision Publications, 2002.

_____. " Gaining perspective on territorial spirits. " In *Deliver Us From Evil: An Uneasy Frontier in Christian Mission,* eds. A. Scott Moreau, Tokunboh Adeyemo, David G., 2002.

Ray, Benjamin C. *African Religions*. Englewood Cliffs, NJ: Prenctice Hall, Inc., 1976.

Richardson, Don. *Peace Child*. Glendale, Calif.: Regal Books, 1976.

Stott, J.R.W and R. Coote (eds.), *Down to Earth: Studies in Christianity and Culture.* Grand Rapids: Eerdmans. 1980.

Sawyerr, Harry, *Sacrifice. In Biblical Revelation and African Beliefs,* eds. Kwesi A. Dickson and Paul Ellingworth, 57-82. London: Lutterworth Press, 1969.

Skarsaune, Oskar and Tormod Engelsviken, "Possession and exorcism in the history of the church," In *Deliver Us From Evil: An Uneasy Frontier in Christian Mission,* eds. A. Scott, 2000.

Taylor, John V. *The Primal Vision*. Philadelphia: Fortress Press, 1963.

Thomas, Juliet, "Issues from the Indian perspective." In *Deliver Us From Evil: An Uneasy Frontier in Christian Mission,* eds. A Scott Moreau, Tokunboh Adeyemo, David G, 2000.

Tippett, A. R. *Solomon Islands Christianity* . New York: Friendship Press, 1967.

Van Rheenen, Gailyn. *Communicating Christ in Animistic Contexts.* Pasadena: William Carey Library, 1991.

Van Rheenen, Gailyn, "Spiritual Warfare," in *Missions Dictionary*, 2003. http://www.missiology.org/missionsdictionary.htm.

Zwemer, Samuel N. *The Influence of Animism on Islam*. New York: Macmillan, 1920.

CHAPTER 3

Syncretistic Worldview

The previous lecture focused on the Animistic Worldview. Today we consider the issue of Syncretistic Worldviews. We begin by defining the term "syncretism."[51] We will then discuss the factors that contribute to syncretism and we will conclude with a presentation of contemporary examples of syncretism.

Definition of the Term Syncretism

In the encyclopedia edited by Dr. Miguel De La Torre entitled, *"Hispanic American Religious Cultures,"* the author gives a historical summary of the use of the term "syncretism." He explains:

> The earliest use of the term "syncretism" occurred when Plutarch chose it to describe how the Cretans would quarrel among themselves but quickly reconciled with foreign enemies. By the sixteenth century, Erasmus used the term to describe the reconciliation achieved among those who theologically disagreed. The term came to imply the mixture of ideas or concepts–especially religious ideas and concepts. Today, the term is mainly used among religious thinkers to describe a mixture of fusion of a "pure" religious faith with a "pagan" religion.[52]

In his chapter entitled "Christopaganism or Indigenous Christianity," Alan R. Tippett confirms the origin of the term "syncretism" and defines it:

> I believe that the etymological derivation of the Word takes us back to political events in early Crete where two parties coalesced (*sunkretizo*) thus giving birth to a noun meaning the union of opposites (two Cretan parties united against a third, forming a new unit, *sunkretismos*) hence "syncretism" as defined above.[53]

> Syncretism may be defined as the union of two opposite forces, beliefs, systems, or tenets so that the united form is a new thing, neither one nor the other.[54]

The Dictionary of the Spanish Language of the Royal Spanish Academy (Diccionario De La Lengua Española, Real Academia Española) defines syncretism as, "A philosophical system that seeks to conciliate different doctrines."[55] In his D*iccionario Hispano Americano De La Misión (Hispanic American Dictionary Of Missions)*, Pablo Deiros describes syncretism as:

> A mixture or combination of beliefs, ideas, practices, or attitudes. This often refers to the mixture of animist beliefs and customs with doctrines, customs and practices of the Roman Catholic Church or the Gospel. It also requires the replacement or elimination of essential truths of the gospel through the incorporation of non-Christian elements from the way of thinking of the person.[56]

Charles H. Kraft defines syncretism as: "The mixing of Christian suppositions with those worldview suppositions that are incompatible with Christianity so that the result is not biblical Christianity."[57] Gailyn Van Rheenen defines syncretism as:

The practice of reformulating beliefs and practices through cultural accommodation to the extent that consciously or unconsciously they harmonize with the dominant culture… the result that Christianity loses its distinctive nature and speaks with a voice that reflects the culture .[58]

As shown in these definitions, syncretism encompasses more than a mixture of beliefs and concepts. This term also includes the mixture of customs and practices and therefore the elimination of essential truths of the gospel as the incorporation of non-Christian elements. This syncretism can penetrate a worldview both consciously and unconsciously. This mixture results in a Christianity that is not faithful to the teachings of the Word of God.

Factors Contributing to Syncretism

A number of factors contribute or cause syncretism among the people receiving the message of the Gospel in different cultures. These causes are:

- Partial conversion,

- Discipleship that is not contextualized,

- Inadequate contextualization in training of leaders,

- The importation of faith expressions in spiritual and human factors.

Partial Conversion

With the term "partial conversion," we mean that because the gospel has not been explained in a clear and substantial manner, some people make a decision to "receive Christ" without understanding the implications of that decision. The writers of the report "Willowbank" emphasize the need to understand the radical nature of conversion. They explain:

> We are convinced that the radical nature of conversion to Jesus Christ needs to be re-affirmed in the contemporary church.... The conversion involves as well a break with the past so complete that is spoken of in terms of death. We have been crucified with Christ. Through his cross we died to the godless world, its outlook, and its standards. We also "put off" like a soiled garment the old Adam, our former and fallen humanity. And Jesus warned us that this turning away from the past may involve painful sacrifices, even the loss of family and possessions (e.g., Luke 14:25).[59]

One of the dangers in communicating the gospel message to persons in animistic cultures is that they might think that receiving Christ means only adding him to their collections of gods that they already have without rejecting the anti-biblical beliefs and practices. In the book of Joshua the decision is clear, *"Choose you this day whom you will serve...."* *(24:14)*. To prevent syncretism, Christian witnesses must present the whole gospel in a manner that takes into account people's worldview. Van Rheenen stresses this truth when he writes:

Often the gospel has been presented in a partial manner and has not had active contact with the dominant themes of the local culture. In the words of Christ to Paul (Acts 26:18) there has very often been only a partial "eye opening" to perceive the wonderful works of God in Jesus Christ. There had been a "conversion from darkness to light" "from the power of Satan to God..." The full dimension of the Gospel has not had an adequate contact with the culture.[60]

Syncretism is much less likely to happen when the whole Gospel is presented in an understandable way and people are led to biblical conversion experiences.

No Contextualized Discipleship

What Van Rheenen says about communicating the Gospel applies to discipleship. In many cases imported discipleship methods have been used that, to be sure, deal with important subjects (e.g., prayer, Bible reading, etc.,) but not with the issues that people face in their daily lives related to animistic beliefs and practices. This failure to deal with the previous Animistic realities often results in people identifying themselves as "Christian" yet secretly going to healers or diviners to seek solutions to their problems. Obviously an urgent need to design contextualized discipleship models exists.

Inadequate Contextualization In Leadership Training

In his book, *Solomon Islands Christianity*, Allan R. Tippett, after a careful study of independent movements, concludes that when a Mission (group of missionaries) fails to produce an indigenous Church the result is going to be a syncretistic movement. He explains that when there are significant deficiencies in the indigenous instruction of the pastors, the movement tends to be syncretistic.

Van Rheenen expressed concern about non-contextualized instruction. He explains:

> Following Western models of thought Christianity is too frequently communicated on the cosmological level without dealing with everyday issues of daily life. Western Christianity is greatly concerned with questions concerning the origins (From where have we come? How have we become what we are?); from destiny (Where are we heading?) and the ultimate meaning of life (What is the ultimate purpose of existing?). In most of the rest of the world, however, people are more concerned with practical, everyday issues such as illness, death, drought, financial success and romance ... The end result is frequently a split level Christianity. New Christians follow the way of Christ on the cosmological level but use traditional ways of thinking when dealing with everyday problems.[61]

The syncretism that stems from the lack of an indigenous church that addresses the genuine needs of the people as they struggle with the traditional problems while striving to live in the new faith can be alleviated by proper leadership training. When the church leaders understand the changing nature of biblical conversion the tendency to revert to older patterns of life among the people are lessened. Thus, a way to avoid syncretism in the lives of the Christians is better training for their leaders.

Imported Expressions of Faith

Charles Kraft believes that two paths lead to syncretism. He explains:

> But there are at least two paths to syncretism. One is by importing foreign expressions of the faith and allowing the receiving people to attach their own worldview suppositions to these practices with little or no guidance from the missionaries. The result is a kind "nativistic Christianity" or even, as in Latin America, "Christ-Paganism." Roman Catholic missionaries especially have fallen into this trap by assuming that when people practice so called "Christian," rituals and use "Christian" terminology, they mean to them the same thing that European Christians mean.
>
> The other way to syncretism is to so dominate a receiving people's practice of Christianity that both the surface-level practices and the deep-level suppositions are imported. The result is a totally foreign, un-adapted kind of Christianity that requires the people to worship and practice their faith according to foreign patterns and to develop a set of worldview suppositions for church situations that are largely ignored in the rest of their lives. Their traditional worldview, then, remains almost untouched by biblical principles.[62]

Human and Spiritual Factors

In addition to considering the missiological factors, it is important to recognize that there are also spiritual and human factors that can contribute to syncretism. Under the spiritual factors we have to include the work of Satan. The analogy that Jesus gave about the house that is possessed by spirits but remains empty and is possessed by even more spirits (Matt 12:43-45), gives an indication of the persistent work of Satan. As mentioned in the chapter on animism, new believers need to learn how to triumph in confrontations with the enemy.

In terms of human factors, a tendency remains to continue a connection with the past. Consciously or unconsciously people tend to retain suppositions and beliefs even though they have adopted a new faith. It is interesting to note that most of the Judaizers that caused so much trouble to the apostle Paul were *"Pharisees who had been converted"* (Acts 15:5). Apparently they had received Christ as their Messiah but had retained at least some of the suppositions of their sect.

This is not a complete list of the factors contributing to syncretism. As we have seen, there are external and internal factors that contribute to syncretism. Even with good reason several of these factors are attributed largely to the work of missionaries and workers with a Western worldview, it is important to note that due to the fact that many missionaries are being sent from countries that were recipients of the gospel message they are likely to make the same mistakes in the countries to which they are sent. These errors can be made in cross-cultural work within the same country.

Contemporary examples Syncretism

Unfortunately, throughout the world there are many examples of syncretism. Due to lack of time and space and being that we are presenting these lectures in a Latin American country, we will present three examples of syncretism in this region of the world. These are examples of syncretism in Catholicism (Popular Religiosity), Santeria, and Protestantism.

Popular Religiosity

Many persons who identify themselves as "Latin Americans" and "Catholics" practice what has been called "Popular Religiosity." This type of devotion is also known as "Popular Catholicism, popular piety, popular devotion, *sensus fidelium*, and popular religiosity." As Gilberto Cavazos-González states, the Catholic Church has recognized and promoted the practice of popular religiosity. He explains:

> Recognizing that Christian spirituality is nourished not only by the Sacred Liturgy of the universal Church, in its Constitution on the Liturgy (*Sacramentum Concillum* (12-13) the Second Vatican Council (1963) encourages the use of what it calls popular devotions, pious exercises, and religious practices of local churches.[63]

Even though the Second Vatican Council supported religiosity, the Latin American Episcopal Council in Medellín, Colombia (1968) warned against popular religiosity which consists mainly of "promises, pilgrimages, untold devotions based on the sacraments that also have to do more with social activities than with the genuine Christian life."[64]

Cavazos-Gonzalez states that Pope Paul VI in 1975 wrote an Apostolic Exhortation *Evangelli nuntiandi* in which he supported popular religiosity as a way toward "a genuine encounter with God in Jesus Christ" (EN 48).[65]

The Catholic Church support of popular religiosity is evident in the devotion to Mary. The Second Vatican Council document entitled *Lumen Gentium*, affirms the cult to Mary:

> The sacred synod teaches this Catholic doctrine and at the same time carefully admonishes the children of the church to worship, especially the liturgical cult, of the Blessed Virgin be generously fostered, and that the practices and exercises of devotion towards her, recommended by authoritative teaching of the church in the course of the centuries is highly esteemed, and that those decrees which were given in primitive times about the cult of images of Christ, of the Virgin and of the saints, be observed religiously.[66]

The cult of Mary mixed with local traditions is seen in different forms throughout Latin America. In Mexico there is the veneration of the Virgin of

Guadalupe. This tradition is based on the alleged apparition of the Virgin Mary in 1531 A.D. to Juan Diego in Tepeyac, the place where the Indians worshiped the goddess Tonantzin. According to this tradition, the image of Mary was miraculously engraved on the cape that Juan Diego was wearing and continues to be an object of adoration to this day. Cavazos-Gonzalez explains:

> To the Nahuatl mind it seems to be a reference to the goddess Coatlicue (Skirt of serpents) who as Tonantzin (our mother) used to appear on Tepeyac and who is the virgin mother of the god Quetzalcoatl (Feathered serpent) whose return they awaited. To the Spanish Christian mind of the late Middle Ages, it seems to be reference to Genesis 3:15 which in the Vulgate had been mistranslated as "she (ipsa) shall crush your (snake) head," rather than he (*ipsum*) referring to the woman's offspring. Bishop Zumarraga believed that "Coatlaxopueh" was a mispronunciation of Guadalupe, a title by which Mary was revered in Extremadura, Spain. As a result, our Lady Tepeyac is usually recognized as Guadalupe.[67]

She utilized the name "Coatlaxopeuh" (pronounced *quatlashupe*) to refer to herself and the native interpretation, in contrast with the Spanish interpretation, reflects a mixture of meanings related to the devotions to Mary. This mixture is also seen in the characteristics that the devoted attribute to Mary. One of these is the spirituality of women in most traditional religions. Nestor Medina explains:

> In many places the Earth Mother or the Pachamama has been replaced with devotion to

Mary. In other places the Pachamama is portrayed with Marian overtones. As Diego Irarrázabal says, "Mary has been *Pachamanized* and its communities have been Marianized."[68]

Mary is known by different names throughout Latin America. Cavazos Gonzalez provides a list:

- Our Lady of Lujan; Argentina

- The Virgin of Copacabana, Bolivia

- The Appeared One, Brazil

- Our Lady of Carmen; Chile

- Our Lady of Chiquinquirá ; Colombia

- Holy Mary of the Angels; Costa Rica

- Our Lady of Charity; Cuba

- Virgen of Peace, El Salvador

- Our Lady of Quinche; Ecuador

- Holy Mary of Pilar; Spain

- The Virgin of the Rosary, Guatemala

- Our Lady of Conception; Honduras

- Virgin of the Old; Nicaragua

- Our Lady of Antigua; Panamá

- Our Lady of Caacupé; Paraguay

- The Virgin of Mercy; Peru

- Our Lady Mother of Divine Providence; Puerto Rico

- Our Lady of Altagracia; Dominican Republic

- The Virgin of the Thirty-Three; Uruguay

- Lady of Coromoto; Venezuela.[69]

In these pages we will deal with these devotions to Mary as a group rather than individually. These popular devotions include processions, pilgrimages, vows, sacrifices, fiestas, and an untold number of practices that reflect a mixture of native meanings with those of Catholicism. Even though Roman Catholic theologians make a distinction between "worship" and "veneration," the truth of the matter is that many of the people that participate in the acts of devotion to Mary see them as worship. Ignacio Manuel Altamirando expresses this when he says: "The day that the Virgin of Tepeyac is not worshiped in this country, it is a certain thing that not only will Mexican nationality disappear but even the memories of the dwellers of today's Mexico."[70]

These expressions of devotion to Mary are not just the practice of two parallel religions but a mixture of worldviews of both, therefore, a syncretism. Nestor Medina affirms:

> It would be a mistake to conclude that these are simply contextual expressions and appropriations

57

of devotion to Mary the Mother of Jesus. Although there are Christian elements in each of the various Marys venerated by the people, a careful analysis of their origins and development reveals that these are the amalgam of indigenous and European religious elements.[71] Negatively understood as syncretistic, these new expressions are specific ways in which the indigenous people adopted, adapted, and reinterpreted Christian elements without fully abandoning their primal inherited religious practices. The claim that many indigenous peoples have "converted' to Christianity should not be understood as a rejection of their primal religious worldview.[72]

Santeria

Santeria is an expression that requires a different category from the others. Miguel de la Torre states that "among Latinos/as, the term syncretism is mainly used to describe non-Christian faith traditions that use Christian symbols, concepts, and ideas, specifically *Santería*, but also other traditions with indigenous roots like *curanderismo* or *espiritismo*.[73]

Donald Moore defines Santeria as:

It is an Afro-Caribbean religion that combines animistic and pantheistic aspects with the worship of ancestors and the Cuban Catholicism. It is a syncretistic religion that mixes the belief in the orishas, or gods of the Yoruba pantheon, a town southwest of Nigeria, with Catholic saints. At times it is identified as the religion of the orichas.[74]

The worldview of those who practice Santeria is based on the pre-Christian faith Lukumi-Yoruba and not based on Christianity or the Bible. Nestor Medina gives a detailed explanation of this worldview:

> Lukumí–Yoruba is a pre-Christian faith that does not rely on Christianity or the Bible. It believes in one almighty creator God known as "Olodumare" and a hereditary core of deified emissaries named orishas that have delegated or borrowed power.... Core beliefs include a concept of reincarnation the fulfillment of the destiny assigned by Olodumare. Human reason and purpose are conceptualized within a framework connected with nature, of Olodumare's planetary creation, free will and fate, universal laws and the recognition of binary principles constructive and destructive forces that may be natural or supernatural. The beliefs include the sacredness of a small group of sacrificial animals that form an integral part of Olodumare's mandates.... This religion has no concept of the Christian Satan or Devil power authority or concept of hell. The philosophy focuses the here and now-balance and the resolution of life's trials and tribulations. It is not based on the idea of miracle or life after death paradise. Central to the core beliefs is that Olodumare distributed knowledge; therefore, all religions have truth but none hold a monopoly on truth.[75]

Santeria includes a large number of myths, stories, legends (patakí) that give a reason for existence to many of their ceremonies and customs and makes them more understandable. Even though there are more than 400 divinities, and sixteen are worshipped actively,[76] the ones that provide the principal base are Obatalá, Ochún, Yemayá, Oyá, Changó and the Guerreros who are Elewá, Ogún, Ochosi y Ozún. In connection with these orichas who are deities and saints, rites of initiation, divination and magic are celebrated.[77]

The syncretism of Santería consists of the coupling of the Catholic saints with pagan deities. Donald Moore gives a summary of this:

> For the santero, the person recognized by this religion of orichas, the deities are supernatural entities and emanations of **Olofi**, the God of human beings and saints. The gods have two characteristics, one is the control of a variety of efforts, endeavors and human interests and the other is the representation of different elements or forces of nature. Some of sixteen that are worshipped are:

- **Obatalá**, represented by the Catholic saint Virgin of the Mercies, is the father of the orichas, the patron saint of peace and purity.

- **Orunla**, also known as **Ifá** and **Orúnmila**, is the patron of the priests (**babalawos**) and the main diviner of the Yoruba pantheon. He is represented by the Catholic Saint Francis of Assisi.

- **Yemayá**, the patron of the seas and of maternity because she is the First mother of humanity, is the mother of fourteen of the most important orichas, including Changó. She is usually represented by the Virgen de Regla.

- **Ochún**, the younger sister of Yemayá, the only owner of love, of marriage, of gold and of the rivers is the favorite concubine of Changó. She is represented by the Virgin of Caridad del Cobre, the patron saint of Cuba.

- **Oyá**, the queen of the dead, owner of the flame and patron of the cemetery, is one of the favorite lovers of Changó is the daughter of Yemayá and us usually represented by Santa Teresa and the Virgin de la Candelaria. She is known in Puerto Rico as the land of Oyá .

- **Changó**, la divinity of de la virility, the patron of fire, the lightning and thunder give victory over the enemies and troubles. This son of Yemayá is represented with the image of Santa Bárbara. He committed incest with his mother and has three other women including Ochún and Oyá .

- Four deities form the group identified as **the Warriors.** They are Elew á (Elegua, Elegu á, o Eleggu á), Ogún, Ochosi y Ozún. **Elewá** is the guardian of the doors including the one of the dead and the messenger of Olofi the other orichas. Without him, nothing can be accomplished. He is the deity of divination and of the santero. He is usually represented by the Catholic saint *San Antonio* and the *Niño de Praga* or *de Atocha*. Additionally he is represented with another image: a stone that has the form of a head and us usually placed behind the door of the houses.

- **Ogún**, a son of Yemayá is represented by the image of Saint Peter, is the patron of metals and of every working person.

- **Ochosi**, a son of Yemayá, represented by the image of San Norberto, is the patron saint of hunters.

- **Ozún**, the oricha that is always accompanied by Elewá, warns santeros when danger is approaching. His representation is the image of Saint John the Baptist.[78]

The attraction for many to Santeria is divination. Through this practice, people think they can choose a better life, change their destiny in this life, and improve their health, love, and money. What gives a sense of security to many people is that this is done under the alleged approval of the Catholic saints. The mixture of syncretism is so subtle that practitioners do not know when they are transitioning from one another.

Syncretism in Protestantism

Evangelicals tend to think that syncretism happens in other religious traditions but not in theirs. The fact is that syncretism can and does occur in all settings due to the fact that, with the exception of totally isolated tribes, there is always a variety of worldviews in areas where people are born and grow. Gailyn Van Rheenen asserts that in his own American culture there is the danger of syncretism:

> Syncretism develops because the Christian community attempts to make its message and life attractive, alluring, and appealing to those outside the fellowship. Over a period of years the

accommodations become routinized, integrated into the narrative story of the Christian community and inseparable from its life. When major worldview changes occur within the dominant culture, the church has difficulty separating the eternals from the temporals. The church tends to lose her moorings because she has for too long been swept along with the ebb and flow of cultural currents. Syncretism thus occurs when Christianity opts into the major cultural suppositions of its society (Van Rheenen 1997).

For example, in my home country there have been two vastly different worldview types, theism and secularism, intertwined in the souls of the average Christians and competing for their allegiance. North American Christians acknowledge God and desire to be faithful to him. They believe that God sent Jesus to die for them and live with hope that they will ultimately live with God in heaven. At the same time they have a great belief in human abilities through science to solve all human problems. They tend to divide the world into two large slices, the natural and the supernatural. Only natural powers, which can be empirically analyzed, are thought to operate in the natural world. Thus Christians often seek medicine and therapy for illness without relying on the Great Physician. In other words, prayer and healing are divorced as if God has little to do with life. Many study the sciences without reflecting on the Creator who sustains the universe. Science and religion are thus disconnected. This can lead to the belief that humanity, with its scientific understanding, is self-sufficient, able to handle all obstacles in life, and does not need God.[79]

Kraft gives an example of a similar attitude when he states: "In America it is syncretistic un-biblical Christianity that sees "the American way of life" as identical with biblical Christianity or assumes that, by generating enough faith we can pressure God into giving us whatever we want...."[80]

In addition to the syncretism that occurs as a result of mixing of the deistic and naturalistic worldviews, there are types of syncretism that are a mixture of deistic and animistic worldviews. In such settings it is helpful to ask the question, how many of the suppositions continue to be part of the thinking when people with an animistic background make a decision to receive Christ? One way to know the answer is to analyze how many animistic practices continue to have influence in the lives of believers.

For example, how many are still influenced by such as evil eye, evil air, cleansing, cure from fright, luck, destiny, day of the dead, veneration of the dead, fetishes, and other animistic practices? How many believers even secretly go to traditional healers or diviners when they have illness or problems? How many have a concept of prayer as if it were a magic that can be manipulated (control) using prescribed formulas or phrases to get what they want rather than submit to the will of God?

Syncretism within worldviews can be both subtle and devastating. The main danger is that it can give the person a false confidence about his relationship with God and his eternal future. In addition, syncretism can undermine the spiritual growth of believers, deprive them of a sense of victory in their lives, and undermine their evangelistic ministry with people who are still in spiritual darkness. The more we understand the types of syncretism and their effects on the people to whom we minister the better we are going to be in empowering them to live victorious lives.

Reflection

1. Gilberto Cavazos González affirms that the leaders in Institutional Catholicism and Protestantism do not need to be afraid of popular religiosity. "It is not a problem to be resolved but a blessing to be appreciated." What is your opinion about this statement?

2. What examples of syncretism have you observed in the communities where you have lived? What examples of syncretism have you observed among people who practice traditional, Catholic, and Evangelical religions?

3 One of the causes of syncretism that has been mentioned is the partial conversion of people. What evangelization plan could you design (including concepts that are going to be taught and practices that are going to be established to meet this need?

4 Another of the causes of syncretism that has been mentioned is the un-contextualized training of leaders. What training plan could you design (including concepts that are going to be taught and practices that are going to be established to meet this need)?

5   Van Rheenen mentions exaggerated accommodation as one of the factors that contribute to syncretism. Is it reasonable to think that a certain degree of contextualization (accommodation) is needed so that the message might be understood and put into practice? What principles would you follow in designing a contextualized strategy for a church in which you serve?

Bibliography

Ayorinde, Christine. *Revolution and National Identity*. Gainesville: University Press of Florida, 2004.

Brown, David H. *Santería Enthroned Art, Ritual, and Innovation in an Afro-Cuban Religion*. Chicago: The University of Chicago Press, 2003.

Canizares, Raúl. *Cuban Santería: Walking with the Night*. Destiny Press, 1999.

Miguel de la Torre. *Santería the Beliefs and Rituals of a Growing Religion in America*. Grand Rapids, MI: Wm. B. Eerdmans Publishing Co. 2004.

Dobson, Jualynne E. Sacred *Space and Religious Traditions in Oriente Cuba*. University of New Mexico Press, 2000

Mason, Michael Atwood. *Living Santería Rituals and Experiences in an Afro-Cuban Religion*. Washington, DC: Smithsonian Institution Press, 2002.

Murphy, Joseph. *Working the Spirit: Ceremonies of the African Diaspora*. Boston: Boston Beacon Press, 1994.

Mercedes Cross Sandoval. *The Orichas and Santería : Africa to Cuba and Beyond*. Florida University, 2006

CHAPTER 4

Monotheistic Worldview

In this chapter we discuss two monotheistic worldviews: The Muslim and the Christian.[81] In order to have a better understanding of the Muslim worldview we are going to start with a brief description of the writing of the *Qur'an*. We then focus on the basic suppositions of the Muslim worldview after which we will discuss the basic suppositions of the Christian worldview. From that vantage we will study the barriers and bridges to be taken into account in communicating the gospel in a Muslim context.

The Writing of the *Qur'an*

The writing of the *Qur'an* is interwoven with the person and work of Muhammad ibn Abdullah who was born in 570 AD in Mecca. Mecca at that time was one of the most important cities of Arabia and the center of animism and idolatry. Muhammad was orphaned at an early age (his father, Abd Allá, died before Muhammad was born and his mother died when he was 6 years old). Brought up by his uncle (Abu Talib), Muhammad traveled throughout Syria and Palestine where he had contact with Jews and Christians.[82] At the age of 25, he married Khadija, a rich widow.

In the year 622, Muhammad fled (his *hegira*) his city, Mecca, to escape his persecutors, and established a theocratic community (*ummah*) in Medina, at the time called Uthrim. In the year 624 Muhammad and his armies returned to the city of Mecca.[83]

At 35 years old, Muhammad, who was unhappy with the moral and social conditions in Arabia, began to have visions. In the year 610, a night that Muslims commemorate as the "Night of Power and of Excellence," Muhammad said that he received the first message or revelation (which tradition says was revealed by the angel Gabriel). The *Qur'an*, Surah (Chapter) 96 contains his First vision and calling to be a prophet.[84] During the following twelve years Muhammad claimed that he continued having visions in which he received the content of the *Qur'an*. Mohammad recited the vision material and his wife and other followers transcribed the words from his dictation.

The Muslim Worldview

In a certain sense it cannot be said that there is only one Muslim worldview due to the fact that "Muslims are divided into hundreds of homogeneous units which differ one from the other geographically, ethnically, ideologically, and often theologically."[85] "Religiously Muslims are divided into Shias, Sunnis, Bahais, Ismailis, Ahl-i-Haqq, Yezdis, communists, secularists, and both progressive and conservative Muslims."[86] However, there are several basic suppositions in the Muslim worldview which can be identified and analyzed. In addition to the basic suppositions, there are specific doctrines that Muslims have in common. In this section we will focus our attention on the suppositions of both worldviews.

Basic Suppositions

Several basic suppositions in Islam define their worldview. These basic suppositions include the nature of Allah, human nature, divine guidance, and submission.

The Nature of Allah

One Muslim supposition says that *Allah* is totally different from other beings. The *Qur'an* states: *"(He is) the Creator of the heavens and earth; He has made for you pairs from among yourselves, and pairs among the cattle; by this does He multiply you; therefore there is nothing whatever like unto Him, and He is the one who hears and sees (all things)"* (Surah 42:11). An implication of this supposition is the *Allah* cannot be known.[87] The teaching indicates that people can know something about *Allah* but cannot know Him as a person. The idea is that *Allah* reveals His will but not Himself to His people.[88]

Another implication of the Muslim worldview is that there is not an analogical relation between *Allah* and people. In other words, there is nothing in the Muslim worldview that indicates that human beings were created in the image of *Allah*.[89] Therefore, the

Muslim worldview believes in the absolute transcendence of Allah.

The Muslim worldview presents *Allah* in a very literal and absolute sense. The essential quality of *Allah* is power. This worldview uses 99 names (attributes) to *Allah*-73 are in the *Qur'an*, and 26 in the *Hadith*. The word "saint" is attributed to God only once in the *Qur'an* and involves a title that is more formal than moral. "Allah is He, than Whom there is no other god; - the Sovereign and Holy One, the Source of Peace (and perfection), the Guardian of Faith, the Preserver of Safety, the Exalted in Might, the Irresistible, and the Supreme: Glory to Allah! (High is He) above the partners they attribute to him" (59:23).[90] His love is one of an owner toward his servant, reciprocal, not unconditional (11:92; 85:14).

Human Nature

The Muslim supposition about human nature is that people are basically "good" and "pure." The *Qur'an* says: "We have indeed created man in the best of moulds" (Surah 95:4). The *Qur'an* admits that Adam was weak and forgetful: "We had already, beforehand, taken the covenant with Adam, but he forgot; and We found on his part no firm resolve" (Surah 20: 115). Samuel P. Schlorff explains:

> In the qur'anic account of Adam and Eve, they did not intend to disobey, they simply "forgot" God's command. And after Adam sinned, God "relented" and "forgave" him, promised him "guidance" and assured him he had "nothing to

fear" provided he followed that guidance (Surah 20:115-127).[91]

Dr. Samuel Shahid gives a similar explanation of the Muslim worldview regarding Adam and Eve:

> Muslims believe that man is born innocent. The Qur'an records the story of the of Adam and Eve's disobedience. It is similar to the biblical account, but the consequences of their actions differ from the Bible. The Qur'anic text indicates that God expelled Adam and Eve out of the Garden of Eden because of their disobedience, but they repented and God accepted their repentance. Muslims do not believe that Adam and Eve's sin corrupted human nature. They do not believe that Adam's sin was passed on to others causing all to sin and fall short of the glory of God.[92]

According to this Muslim supposition human beings do not have a sinful nature because they have not had a moral failure. If they are separated from Allah it is because of His transcendence and not because of the sins of humanity. What men need is not salvation but direction.

The Divine Guidance

Another of the basic Muslim suppositions is expressed as "divine guidance." A central idea regarding this supposition is that *Allah* has provided the guidance that people need. Schlorff explains:

> Guidance" (*hudá*) is one of the central themes of the Qur'an; the verb form of this root alone occurs some two hundred times, and the noun form 85

71

times, not to mention similar terms and ideas. Guidance is said to be found in "the Torah and the Gospel" (Surah 3:2, etc.), but above all in the Qur'an it is called "a guidance and mercy for believers" (e.g., 27:77). The Qur'an, together with the traditions (*Hadiths*) concerning what Muhammad said and certain other sources, constitute the Religious Law (*Shari'ah*) which Muslims believe to be the very law of God.[93]

Nurtured in the concept of divine guidance is the concept of predestination. Several portions of the *Qur'an* clearly teach the concept of predestination. These include the following:

"We have created all things in proportion and measure" (Surah 54:49).

"But Allah has created you and your handiwork" (Surah 37: 96).

"For we assuredly sent amongst every People a Messenger, (with the Command) 'Serve Allah and eschew Evil': of the people were some whom Allah guided, and some on whom Error became established ... "(Surah 16:36).

"This is an admonition: whosoever will, let him take a (straight) Path to his Lord. But you will not, except as Allah wills; for Allah is full of knowledge and Wisdom "(Surah 76:29, 30).

"If We had so willed, We could certainly have brought every soul its true guidance, but the Word from me will come true, I will fill Hell with Jinns and men together" (Surah 32:13).

"Now Allah leaves straying those whom He pleases and guides those whom He pleases. He is Exalted in power, full of Wisdom." (Surah 14:4).

"Would you guide those whom Allah has thrown out of the Way? For those whom Allah has thrown out of the way, you will never find the way "(Surah 4:88).
"If Allah so willed, He could make you all one People, but He leaves straying those whom He pleases, and He guides whom He pleases: but you shall certainly be called to account for all your actions " (Surah 16:93).

From these texts in the *Qur'an* we can deduce the following concepts regarding Allah's guidance. The will of man is totally submitted to the will of *Allah*. He is the creator of the good and the bad. *Allah* may guide or refuse to guide. He can also mislead. He forgives or refuses to forgive according to His will. Whoever *Allah* misguides, none can guide. *Allah* could have made all of humanity into one people (*umah*). He misguides people; people are responsible for the consequences.[94]

The clear impression one gets from reading this is that the Muslim worldview perceives the observance of the law as a way to obey *Allah*, but it is *Allah* who determines the fate of people.

Submission

The main idea of submission is the principle that integrates everything in a coherent system that is found in the world *"Islam."* Schlorff gives an explanation about the use and meaning of the term:

It is an Arabic word that Muslims love to use and it means "submission," while the term *Muslim means* "one who submits." The corresponding verb (*aslama*) means to "make peace," "surrender," or "submit." It is typically used to mean the vanquished laying down their swords before the vector. The word expresses the Islamic ideal that every aspect life, of the individual, or of society should be lived in submission to God.[95]

This submission is expressed in an individual sense and is particularly seen in the "five pillars" of Islam. The first pillar is the confession of faith. The recitation of the creed indicates that one has understood, appreciated, and internalized the theology of the message.... The second pillar is prayer. This can be seen when the Muslim ceases his activities five times a day to pray. The third pillar is almsgiving. The fourth is the practice of fasting during Ramadan. The fifth pillar is the pilgrimage to Mecca. At least once in his life the Muslim should make the effort to go to Mecca the birth place of Muhammad.[96]

The communal expression of submission should be the formation of a community.

The first community in Medina is considered to be the model "community of submission" of all time – the exemplar which Muslims from thereafter strive to emulate ... The model requires a Muslim government to provide social and legal framework necessary to facilitate the submission to the law. There is no separation between the sacred and the secular, between church and state. This community is one, universal and cohesive, representing for Muslims the Kingdom of God on earth.[97]

This supposition explains the effort of certain groups of Muslims to establish this type of government in the world.

The Christian Worldview

The observation we made about the Muslim worldview we make about the Christian worldview. Usually it is not advisable to use the term "Christian" with Muslims. Many associate the term with Catholicism (especially regarding the crusades) or with other groups who call themselves "Christians." Other Muslims do not distinguish between the culture of the Western world (especially American) and the religion that they know as "Christianity." Upon seeing so many negative things in the Western culture they automatically believe that this is due to the fact that Christianity itself is corrupt.

Another reason why some prefer not to use the term "Christian" rests on the fact that the term contains not only theological but also cultural suppositions. Charles Kraft asserts that there are believers in the United States who "see the American way of life as identical with biblical Christianity."[98] Because of this, Kraft insists that there is no such thing as "a single Christian worldview." He explains:

> There are those who speak about of a Christian worldview (e.g., Sire 1976, Schaffer 1976). They are not understanding, however, the all-encompassing nature of worldview in the anthropological sense. They are speaking of the influx of Christian assumptions, values and allegiances into a worldview as if that input constituted the whole worldviews. It does not. Christian Africans, Christian Asian, Christian Europeans and the multitude of committed

Christians of other societies in the world simply do not see most things the same way, despite his commitment to Christ ... There will be certain important similarities. But most of the differences in worldview, as in the surface level cultural behavior, remain - unless, of course, in the process of becoming Christian, these people also change their culture. This latter is not, however, a Christian requirement.[99]

Keeping these caveats in mind, however, from a theological point of view it is possible to identify biblical concepts which are based on suppositions that can be classified as Christian. These basic teachings are going to be called "basic suppositions." After discussing these, we will focus on specific doctrinal issues.

Basic Suppositions

These basic suppositions of the Christian worldview are the person and character of God, human nature, divine guidance, and the community of submission.

The Nature of God

Like the Muslim teaching, the Christian worldview also affirms the transcendence of God. The difference is that, in Christian teaching, God is transcendent but also immanent. Several passages of the Bible clearly state that through the person of Jesus Christ God has made himself known. *"No one has seen God at any time. The only begotten son, who is in the bosom of the Father, He has declared Him* (John 1:18). Jesus said,

"*If you had known me, you would have known my Father also: and from now on you know Him, and have seen Him*" (John 14:7). "*And this is life eternal that they might know thee the only true God, and Jesus Christ whom you have sent*" (John 17:3).

In differentiation from the Muslim worldview, the Christian worldview states that humans were created in the image and God. "*Then God said, let us make man in our image, after our likeness ....*" (Gen 1:26). "*For a man indeed ought not to cover his head, since he is the image and glory of God ....*" (1 Cor 11:7). Also in contrast to the Muslim worldview that says you can know something about God but you cannot know Him personally, the Christian worldview says that you can have knowledge of God and know Him personally. "*And this is eternal life, that they may know You, the only true God, and Jesus Christ whom you have sent .... Now they have known that all things which You have given Me are from You. For I have given to them the words which You have given me; and they have received them, and have known surely that I came from You; and they have believed that You sent Me*" (John 17: 3, 7, 8). Therefore, the Christian worldview affirms the transcendence and immanence of God simultaneously.

Human Nature

The Bible teaches that God created man in a perfect state: "*So God created man in His own image, in the image of God He crested him; male and female He created them*" (Gen 1:27). The Genesis account indicates that there was prefect communion between God and Adam and Eve. Chapter 3 of Genesis, however, says that Adam and Eve disobeyed God and how they were expelled from paradise. Paul explains the effect of sin when he says: *"Therefore, just as sin entered the world through one man, and death through sin, so death passed upon all men because all sinned"* (Rom 5: 12).

The Bible clearly teaches that human beings have a fallen and sinful nature. The remedy is not only seeking God's direction but recognizing their fallen nature, repenting, asking God for forgiveness, and receiving Jesus Christ as the only sacrifice for their sins. The difference between these worldviews is both clear and profound. The Muslim worldview teaches that the person has the moral power to not sin if he seeks the guidance of *Allah*. The Christian Worldview teaches that all humans have sinned (Rom 3:23), that the wages of sin is death but the gift of God is eternal life in Christ Jesus (Rom 6:23). The Christian worldview teaches that no one can reach the will of God in his/her own strength but the Holy Spirit will empower humans to accomplish God's will (2 Pet 1: 2-6).

The Divine Direction

The Christian World has a very different concept from the Muslim worldview on the concept of divine guidance. There is no doubt that the believer receives divine guidance through prayer and the study of the Word of God. However, this direction is not obtained as a result of human effort to fulfill the law of God. The truth is that the Bible clearly teaches that man because of his sinful nature is not able to fulfill the law of God itself. The epistles of the apostle Paul to the Romans, Ephesians, and Galatians clearly explain man's inability of the law to save humanity (Eph 2:8-9). It is very important to keep in mind that in a similar manner to the efforts of law-keeping Jews, Muslims have a legalistic way to try to meet the requirements of *Allah*.

Submission

The idea of submission is also found in the Christian World. Jesus taught his disciples to pray *"Thy will be done as in heaven so in earth"* (Matt 6: 10). Jesus set the example when he prayed in Gethsemane and said, *"Not my will be done but yours be done"* (Matt 26:39). James 4:7 states: *"Therefore submit to God. Resist the devil and he will flee from you."* The submission of the believer to God in all of the spheres of his life is an important supposition in the Christian worldview.

Unlike the Muslim worldview, the Christian worldview does not strive to establish a perfect government here on earth. While Christians should be responsible citizens, the ideal of a perfect community will not be achieved until the believers get to heaven.

Barriers and Bridges

In addition to differences in suppositions between the Muslim worldview and the Christian worldview, there are barriers and bridges that need to be considered in communicating the gospel message to people with Muslim background. In this section we first examine the barriers and then bridges.

Barriers

Certain Christian teachings form definite barriers or difficulties for Muslim belief. Usually, the reasons for the difficulties are not the teachings themselves but the Muslim misunderstanding of the concepts. Barriers (or stumbling blocks) to Muslims are the incarnation of Jesus, the death of Jesus on the cross, and the Trinity.

The Trinity

The Muslim worldview holds that God is absolutely one and indivisible, without equal, without partners, without "people" (Surahs 29:46, 6:22-24, 134-136, 163). The *Qur'an* clearly states: "Do not say "Trinity": Desist: it will be better for you: for Allah is one God: Glory be to Him: (far exalted is He) above having a son." (Surah 4:171). From this perspective of this worldview, many Muslims have the impression that Christians have three gods: God, Jesus, and Mary.[100]

In their zeal to wrestle against polytheism, many Muslims opt for *Allah*, impersonal, mysterious, and unknown. The difficulty with the Muslim worldview is that it proposes a mathematical unity in place of an organic one, an abstract unity in place of one made up of personality.[101] The Muslim understanding of Trinity is not an accurate understanding but forms a definite barrier to their consideration of the Message of Christ.

The Incarnation

For many people with a Muslim worldview it is inconceivable to them that *Allah* has taken a human form. The *Qur'an* affirms categorically that *Allah* does not have a son (Surah 2:110; 6:100; 19:85; 23:91; 112:1-4). The concept in this worldview is that Christ is "a word" from *Allah* and a Spirit from *Allah*, born of the Virgin Mary after Mary received the Spirit of *Allah*, but Christ was never pre-existent. The truth is that the Muslim worldview holds that the *Qur'an* is the Word of God, not created. Warren Chastain explains how deep a barrier the Incarnation is for people with a Muslim worldview. He says:

> We should be able to sympathize with the Muslim's offense at the great stumbling block of the Incarnation. Did God really have to go through all the trouble (as Christians affirm) to deal with some "foibles" or weaknesses of man (the Muslim estimate of sin)? Can the human state be so bad that God must take on human form and come to earth to correct it: Was Jesus' trip necessary? It is inconceivable to the Muslim that God would be humble. And to suggest that God must in some way sacrifice Himself is inconceivable.[102]

George Braswell affirms that the opposition to the doctrine of the incarnation of Jesus is based on the supposition that Muslims have about the nature of Allah. He states:

In truth, in Islam the greatest sin is *shirk,* giving to someone or something even a minimal portion of the sovereignty that belongs to Allah. That is the reason why Muslims cannot accept the Christian belief of the incarnation of God in Jesus.[103]

The Cross

The teaching of the death of Jesus on the cross is another stumbling block for many Muslims. Muslims do not accept the idea that Jesus died on the cross for several reasons. One of the reasons is that their worldview considers the cross a symbol of shame and disgrace that violates the honor of *Allah.*[104] Another reason is that Islam rejects the concept of the fallen nature of man and the principle of the vicarious sacrifice for sin. If you do not believe that man fell into sin, you would see no need for the death of Jesus.

Moreover, the Muslim worldview says that Jesus did not die on the cross. The *Qur'an* states:

> They said (in boast), "We killed Christ Jesus son of Mary, the Messenger of Allah"; - but they did not kill him, nor crucify him, but it was to made to appear to them, and those who differ therein are full of doubt, with no (certain) knowledge, but only conjecture to follow, for of a surety they did not kill him. (Surah 4:157).

Dr. Samuel Shahid explains the belief of Muslims regarding the crucifixion of Jesus:

> Muslims believe that God performed two miracles to save Jesus from being crucified by His enemies. First, God took Jesus to heaven and saved him from his adversaries, and second, God cast the

image of Jesus to the ones who were attacking Jesus, whom they crucified mistakenly in place of Jesus (many believe that Judas Iscariot was mistaken for Jesus). Therefore, Jesus was not crucified, but someone who looked like Jesus. There are Muslims who believe that Jesus was not crucified but died a natural death. Unfortunately Muslims do not go to the genuine source about the crucifixion and do not see the need of Jesus the Redeemer.[105]

Bridges

As there are barriers that hinder the communication of the Gospel to Muslims, so bridges exist that can implement the process of witness. Christians can use these bridges to share with people with a Muslim worldview the message of salvation in Jesus Christ. We will simply mention these bridges.

The Holy Books

The Islamic worldview affirms that there are four sacred books: *Tawrat* (Torh or Pentateuch given to Moses), *Zabur* (Psalms given to David), *Injil* (Gospel given to Jesus), *Qur'an,* (the Scripture given to Muhammad by the angel Gabriel). Question: How many of these "Sacred Books" or portions of them can be used as bridges to communicate the Christian worldview?[106] The fact that Muslims respect Christians as people of a book can also be seen as a bridge to enhance communication between the two groups.

The Prophets

Muslims place great emphasis on the role of the prophets. The *Qur'an* names twenty prophets from Adam, Noah, Abraham and Moses in the Pentateuch, to John and Jesus. George Braswell explains the place of "prophets" in Muslim thinking:

> The Qur'an gives Jesus (called *Isau*) more honorific titles than to any other prophet. He is called Messiah, servant, word, prophet, messenger, sign, mercy, just, blessed close to Allah. A prophet, he is not divine.[107]

Although the Muslim worldview sees all human prophets, *Allah* appointed them to be spokespersons. What are the possibilities of using the teachings of the *Qur'an* about the prophets, especially Jesus, as a bridge to communicate the gospel message?

Last Things

The Muslim worldview expresses great interest in the last things. Braswell says:

> The sense of history is similar to the Jewish and Christian perspectives. From birth until death, life is lived under the law and the judgment of Allah. Beyond death is the resurrection of the dead, the rewards of punishments in paradise and in hell. Islam is very explicit about the end of time. At the trial Allah opens the book of facts. The good and bad deeds are weighed in the balance and the balance determines the fate of the person. Paradise is an eternal garden while hell is a place of fire and horrors. The doctrine of last things in Islam is based on a perspective of omnipotence and

omniscience of Allah. The Qur'an states that Allah has written the entry and exit of every soul and what will happen. Muslims believe that everything comes from Allah and that Allah sends astray whom he wants and correctly guides those whom he wants to. "If Allah wills" is an expression that Muslims use a lot.[108]

In light of these teachings in the Muslim worldviews, how many of these teaches can be used as bridges to communicate the Christian worldview.[109] What strategy would be the most appropriate culturally and spiritually to communicate these truths?

Contextualizing

The fact that there is much diversity among people who identify with the Muslim worldview has led some to devise different strategies to communicate the gospel. John Travis[110] describes a spectrum of six types of "Christ-centered Communities (groups of believers in Christ) that are found in the Muslim world:

C1-Traditional Church Using Outsider Language.[111] Many reflect a western culture. Huge cultural chasm often exists between the church and the surrounding Muslim community.

C2-A Traditional Church Using Insider Language – Essentially the same as C1 except for the language. Though insider language is used, religious vocabulary is probably non- Islamic decisively "Christian." There still remains a cultural gap. Believers call themselves "Christians."

C3-Contextualized Christ-centered Communities Using Insider Language and Religiously Neutral Insider

85

Cultural Forms. Religiously neutral forms may include folk music, ethnic dress, artwork, etc. Islam elements (where present) are "filtered out" so as to use purely "cultural forms." The aim is to reduce foreignness of the gospel and the church by contextualizing to biblically permissible forms. The majority are Muslim background believers.

C4-Contextualized Christ-centered Communities Using Insider Language and Biblically Permissible Cultural and Islamic forms - These forms include praying with raised hands, observing the fast, avoiding eating pork and alcohol and dogs as pets, using the Islamic dress, etc. They identify themselves as followers of Isa the Messiah

C5-Christ-centered Communities of "Messianic Muslims" who have accepted Jesus as Lord and Savior - they remain legally and socially within the Islamic community, accept (or reinterpret) certain aspects of Islamic theology that does not contradict the Bible. They participate in the activities of Muslim prayer and share their faith with Muslims unbelievers. When entire villages accept Christ, they establish Messianic Mosques. The believers are viewed as Muslims by the Muslim community and refer to themselves as Muslims who follow Isa the Messiah.

C6–Small Christ-centered Communities of Secret/Underground believers– They worship Christ secretly (individually of perhaps infrequently in small clusters). Many come to Christ through dreams, visions, miracles, radio broadcasts, tracts, Christian witness while abroad or reading the Bible. On their own initiative. They are perceived as Muslims and identify themselves as Muslims.

Application

A good question is, what are advantages and disadvantages in each of these positions? It would also be good to dialog about each option concerning the position you would adopt if you were doing missionary work among a group of Muslims or another group with similar restrictions. In this type of discussion you should decide how far you can adapt the expression of Christianity without abandoning the basic principles of the Bible. At the same time pay attention to the question, what would happen if there were no types of adaption?

Reflection

1. How do you evaluate Charles Kraft's assertion that there is "not one Christian worldview"?

2. Evaluate the barriers in the Muslim worldview mentioned in this chapter. Indicate how you would respond in order to communicate the Gospel message.

3. Evaluate the bridges to the Muslim worldview and indicate which of these (or what portions of these) you would utilize to communicate the message of salvation.

4. Study carefully the options that John Travis presents in the next section and indicate the strong points and the week points in each option.

Bibliography

Muslim Writers

Ali, A. *The Holy Qur'an* : Text, Translation and Commentary. Washington, DC: The Islamic Center, 1978.

Ajijola, A. *The Myth of the Cross* . Lahore, Pakistan: Islamic
    Publications, 1975.
'Ataur-Rahmin, M. *Jesus Prophet of Islam* . Norfolk, England:
    Diwan Press, 1977.
Hussein, M. *City of Wrong: Friday in Jerusalem* . New York:
    Seabury Press, 1966.
Hussein, A. *On Conviction and Islam* . Cairo: the Supreme Council
    for Islamic Affairs, No publishing date.
Mufassir, S. *Biblical Studies from a Muslim Perspective* .
    Washington, DC: The Islamic Council, 1973.
Shafaat, A. *The Gospel According to Islam* . New York: Vantage
    Press, 1979.

Non-Muslims Writers

Adelphi, G. & Hahn, E. *The Integrity of the Bible According to the
    Qur'an and the Hadit.* Hyderabad, India: Henry Martyn
    Institute of Islamic Studies 1977.
Goldsack, W. *Christ in Islam* . Veppory, Madras: The Christian
    Literature Society, 1905.
Jadeed, I. *The Cross in the Gospel and the Qur'an* . Rikon, Suisse:
    The Good Way.
Lamb, C. *Jesus Through Other Eyes: Christology in Multi-Faith
    Context* . Oxford: Latimer House, 1982.
Parrinder, G. *Jesus in the Qur'an* . New York: Oxford University
    Press.
Robertson, K. (1965), *Jesus or Isa: A comparison of the Jesus of
    the Bible and the Jesus of the Qur'an* . New York: Vantage
    Press.
Wismer, D (1977). *The Islamic Jesus: An Annotated Bibliography
    of Sources in English and French* . New York: Garland.
    Understanding Christian Missions to Islam and Muslims.
"A Look at Islam: Some Beliefs and Practices," SIM Now, 46, July-
    August 1989. Available from SIM USA, 1236 Arrow Pine
    Drive, Charlotte, NC, 28217, USA.

Abdul-Haqq, A. (1980), *Sharing Your Faith with a Muslim* . Minneapolis, MN: Bethany House.

Cooper, A. (ed.) (1985). *Ishmael My Brother: A Biblical Course on Islam*. Bromley, Kent, England: STL Books.

Cragg, K. & Speight, M. (1980),. *Islam from Within: Anthology of a Religion*. Belmont, CA: Wadsworth.

Fry, C. & King, J., (1980), *Islam: a Survey of the Muslim Faith.* Grand Rapids, MI: Baker Books.

Goldsmith, M. (1982). *Islam & Christian Witness* . Downers Grove, IL: InterVarsity Press, 1965.

Jones, L. *Called of God: From Islam to Christ* . Toronto, ON: Fellowship of the Faith for Moslems.

Marsh, C. *Share Your Faith with a Muslim* . Chicago, IL: Moody Press, 1975.

Matheny, T., *Reaching the Arabs: A Felt Need Approach* . Pasadena, CA: William Carey Library, 1981.

Musk, B. *The Unseen Face of Islam* . Eastbourne, E. Sussex, England: Monarch, 1981.

Register, R. *Dialogue and Interfaith Witness with Muslims* . Fort Washington, PA: WEC., 1979. Available from Multi-Language Media, Box 301, Ephrata, PA, 17522, USA (717) 738-0582.

Parshall, P. *New Paths in Muslim Evangelism* : Evangelical Approaches to Contextualization. Grand Rapids, MI: Baker Books, 1980.

Parshall, P. *Bridges to Islam: A Christian Perspective on Folk Islam* Grand Rapids, MI: Baker Books, 1983.

Parshall, P. *Beyond the Mosque* . Grand Rapids, MI: Baker Books, 1985.

Shahid, Samuel. *The Cross or the Crescent: Understanding Islam*, Atlanta: North American Mission Board, 2000, 47.

Shahid, Samuel and Smith, Ebbie C. *Good News for Muslims* (Ft. Worth, TX: Church Starting Network, 2013.

Spencer, H. *Islam and the Gospel of God* . Kashmere Gate, Delhi: ISPCK, 1976.

Watt, M. *Muhammad: Prophet and Statesman*. Oxford, Oxford
University Press, 1961.
Wilson, J. "Moslem Converts." *Moslem World*, 34, 1944, 171-184.

Additional Resources

Eshleman, P. A guidebook to Film Evangelism: A Step-by step
Manual to Accomplish Effective Film Showings and
Follow-up. Laguna Niguel, CA: Campus Crusade for Christ,
1985. Available from the JESUS Film Project, PO Box
7690, Laguna Niguel, CA 92667, USA. (714) 495-7383.
Eshleman, P. *I Just Saw Jesus* San Bernardino, CA: Here's Life,
1985.
Evangelistic Film *Strategy Guide*. San Bernardino, CA: Here's Life
Christian Resource Center, 1984.

CHAPTER 5

The Postmodern Worldview

Probably a more adequate title for this chapter would be "the worldview that postmoderns do not know or do not admit that they have." I suggest this title because in the postmodern period, as David Naugle says, "there is a disbelief that any worldview or large-scale interpretation of reality is true and ought to be believed ad promulgated."[112] One might ask if the disbelief about the ability to understand and describe reality with human language itself may not be a supposition of the postmodern worldview.[113] Or we can ~~ask~~ contemplate the question that Naugle asks: "Does not postmodernism assume a naturalistic worldview as the basis of its assertions?"[114] We are going to develop our reflection on the postmodern worldview by reflecting on questions such as the above. Before beginning a discussion about the Postmodern Worldview, however, we should review two periods prior to postmodern: the pre-modern and modern.

Pre-Modern Worldview

In the pre-modern period "there was substantial confidence on the part of the average Westerner, the Christian in particular, to obtain a comprehensive view of the universe, its facts as well as its values, based on God and his self revelation in the Bible."[115] Millard Erickson explains:

Pre-modern understanding of reality was teleological. There was believed to be a purpose or purposes in the universe, within which humans fit and were to be understood.... In the western tradition, this was the belief that an omnipotent, omniscient God created the entire universe and the human race, and had a plan he was bringing about. [116]

James Sire summarizes the basic suppositions of the theistic, pre-modern Christian

- God is infinite and personal (triune), transcendent and immanent, omniscient, sovereign and good.
- God created the cosmos *ex nihilo* to operate with a uniformity of cause and effect in an open system.
- Human beings are created in the image of God and thus have personality, self-transcendence, intelligence, morality, gregariousness, and creativity.
- Human beings can know both the world around them and God himself because God has built into them the capacity to do so and because he takes an active part in communicating with them.
- Human beings were created good, but through the Fall the image of God became defaced, though not so ruined as not to be capable of restoration; through the work of Christ, God redeemed humanity and began the process of restoration to goodness, though any given person may choose to reject that redemption.
- For each person, death is either the gate to life with God and his people or the gate to eternal separation from the only thing that will ultimately fulfill human aspirations.

- Ethics is transcendent and is base on the character of God as good (holy and loving).
- History is linear, a meaningful sequence of events leading to the fulfillment of god's purpose for humanity.[117]

In summary, the pre-modern worldview was influenced by biblical concepts about God, creation, human beings, earthly life, and preparation for eternal life. Due to confidence in God's revelation in His Word, pre-modern persons held full confidence that the future of mankind was in the hands of the creator of the universe.

Modern Worldview

In the modern period the center of gravity was shifted from God to man, from the Scriptures to science, and from revelation to reason. Modern people believed confidently that human beings, starting with themselves and their own methods of knowing, could obtain an understanding of the universe, at least its realities and values.[118] We can easily observe that along with this transition the focus changed from God to science as the source of truth and the answers to the questions and problems of life. This transition is evident in statements regarding the significant achievements of the past. When the telegraph was invented the first message sent was: "What God has done." When the first astronaut set foot on the moon, his message was: "One small step for man, one giant leap for mankind."

The reality is that many of us grew up with these two worldviews simultaneously. At home (especially evangelicals) grew up with a pre-modern worldview which emphasized our belief in God as our creator, sustainer and Lord. This worldview was reinforced and nurtured in the church fellowship of our brothers and sisters in Christ. At the same time, however, as we pursued our education at school, we not only received academic instruction (reading, math, science, etc.) but began a process of acculturation to the modern worldview with an emphasis on the "scientific method" that included the theory of evolution and the use of reason to solve the problems we face as humans. In this sense we can say we are products of two worldviews: the pre-modern and modern. Today, however we face the additional influence of the postmodern. Before entering a discussion about the postmodern, it is beneficial to do a quick review of the premises of the modern worldview.

The modern worldview is based on a number of suppositions that have influenced western culture for many years. Millard J. Erickson gives a summary of these suppositions.[119]

Naturalism

"Reality is believed to be restricted to the observable system of nature. Its immanent laws are the cause of all that occurs."[120]

Humanism

"Humanism is the highest reality and value, the end for which all reality exists rather than the means to the service of a higher being."[121]

The Scientific Method

"Knowledge is good and can be attained by humans. The method best suited for this enterprise is the scientific method. Observation and experimentation are the sources from which our knowledge of truth is built up."[122]

Reductionism

"From being considered the best means for gaining knowledge, the scientific method came increasingly to be considered the only method, so that various disciplines sought to attain the objectivity and precision of the natural sciences."[123]

Progress

"Because knowledge is good, humanly attainable, and growing, we are progressively overcoming the problems that have beset the human race.[124]

Nature

"Rather than being fixed and static, nature came to be thought of as dynamic, growing and developing. Thus it was able to produce the changes in life forms through immanent processes of evolutions, rather than requiring explanation in terms of a creator and designer."[125]

The Certainty

"Because knowledge is seen as objective, it could attain certainty. This required foundationalism, the belief that it is possible to base knowledge on some sort of absolute first principles. One early model of this was found in the rationalism of René Descartes who found one indubitable belief, namely that he was doubting and then proceeded to draw deductions from that. An alternative was empiricism, the belief that there are purely objective sensory data from which knowledge can be formulated."[126]

Determinism

"There was a belief that what happened in the universe followed from fixed causes. Thus, the scientific method could discover these laws of regularity that controlled the universe. Not only physical events but human behavior was believed to be under etiological control."[127]

Individualism

"The ideal of the knower was the solitary individual, carefully protecting his or her objectivity by weighing all options. Truth, being objective, individuals can discover it by their own efforts."[128]

Anti-authoritarianism

"The human was considered the final and most complete measure of truth. Any externally imposed authority, whether that of the group or of a supernatural being, must be subjected to scrutiny and criticism by human reason."[129]

As seen in this brief summary offered by Erickson, suppositions of modernism emphasize the human ability to know and understand the truth. This knowledge is limited to what one can acquire through reason and experimentation. At the extreme, these suppositions exclude not only the existence but the necessity of a supreme being.

Ed Stetzer assesses the modern worldview saying:

> The system of modernity worked well and served the Western world for two hundred years. In the last few decades, the crack in the wall of modernity began to show... . In other words, at the   of the inevitable progress of the Enlightenment came mustard gas in World War I, Hitler in the Second World War, Mai Lai... Tuskegee, Oklahoma City, and the World Trade Center. The failure of the Enlightenment ideal has led to the new postmodern mood.[130]

David Wells says that modernity "had made extravagant promises about life, liberty, and happiness but in the modern world it had become increasingly difficult to see where those promises were being realized."[131]

In his book, *Christian Belief In A Post Modern World*, Diogenes Allen enumerates four factors that contributed to the breakdown of the modern mentality:

- It has been taken for granted in the intellectual world that the idea of God is superfluous. We do not need God to account for anything.

- The second factor is the failure to find a basis for morality and society. A major project in the Enlightenment was to base traditional morality and society on reason and not on religion.

- The third pillar of the Enlightenment is the belief in inevitable progress. Modern science and technology so improved life that they led to the belief in progress, and in time to belief in inevitable progress.

- The fourth Enlightenment belief that is being questioned is the assumption that knowledge is inherently good. For centuries science has been regarded as unquestionably a force for good... Today we are becoming increasingly aware that there is no inherent connection between knowledge and its beneficial use, with genetic engineering just beginning to open new possibilities of abuse with the power of bombs and other destructive forces at hand. Scientists do not control the use to which knowledge is put, and many even resist taking responsibility for its uses.[132]

- The breaking of the modern mentality has led many to conclude that science has all the answers and that Christianity is intellectually irrelevant to current questions about the existence of the world, the foundation for morality and society and the meaning of life. What relevance does this have for the postmodern mindset? To provide a basis for answering this question we need to give attention to the postmodern worldview.

Postmodern Worldview

Before entering into a discussion about the postmodern worldview it is necessary to define the term "postmodernism." In attempting to give a definition to "postmodernism" we are aware of the fact that as Sire says, "it is difficult to define the undefined." The term is used in so many different facets of cultural and intellectual life by so many people that its meaning often is obfuscated not only in the fringes but at the center.[133] The origin of the use of this term generally is attributed to the field of architecture. When architects decided to abandon the monotonous forms of buildings, as square cement boxes, glass, mirror, and metal, they started to design styles of the past without paying attention to their purpose or original function.[134] This term was popularized when sociologist Jean-François Lyotard used it to indicate a transition in the cultural legitimization.[135] Lyotard defined *postmodernism* as "incredulity toward of meta-narrative."[136] James Sire explains:

> No longer is there a single story, a metanarrative (in our terms a worldview) that holds Western culture together. It is not just that there have long been many stories, each of which gives a binding

power to the social group that takes it as its own. The naturalists have their story, the pantheists theirs, the Christians theirs, ad infinitum. With postmodernism no story may have more credibility than any other. All stories are equally valid, being so validated by the community that lives by them.[137]

Although this term was originally used in the field of sociology, it is now also being used in connection with the discussion of metaphysical, epistemological and ethical in the fields of philosophy, history and theology. Allen makes the observation that postmodernism has made an impact in various branches of knowledge. He explains:

Many have been driven to relativism by the collapse of the Enlightenment's confidence in the power of reason to provide foundation for our truth claims and to achieve finality in our search for truth in the various disciplines. Much of the distress concerning pluralism and relativism which is voiced today springs from a crisis within Christianity itself.[138]

While postmodernism does not emerge from a crisis within Christianity, their suppositions are affecting the thinking of many Christians in our day. Postmodern thinking influences some who hold to the Christian Worldview but who do not have a firm conviction about the exclusivity of Christ as The Savior of the world. In view of this, let us examine briefly the main suppositions of the postmodern worldview.

Postmodern Suppositions

Although there are a number of suppositions which are based on the postmodern worldview, we will limit our discussion to the more widely known concepts that are deeply influencing the thinking of many in our day.

Uncertainty regarding knowledge

In postmodern thought, the first question is not what is there or how we know what is there but how language functions to construct meaning.[139] In his deconstruction of logo centrism, Jacques Derridá expresses doubts about the ability of language to represent reality accurately and objectively. He says, "Thus, worldviews once deconstructed, are reduced to a self-referential system of linguistic signifiers dispossessed of any authentic metaphysical, epistemological, or moral import."[140]

Terry Eagleton claims that the Western mind has been perennially logocentric and has maintained a persistent search to find the ultimate that serves as the secure foundation of all thought, language, and human experience. He explains describes the Western mind:

> It has yearned for the sign which will give meaning to all others – the "transcendental signifier" – and for the anchoring, unquestionable meaning to which all our signs can be seen to point (the "transcendental signified" A great number of candidates for this role - God, the idea, the World Spirit, the Self, substance, matter, and on and on - have thrust themselves from time to

time. Since each of these concepts hopes to found our whole system of thought and language, it ᐧ must itself be beyond that system, untainted by its play of linguistic differences. It cannot be implicated in the very language which it attempts to order and anchor.[141]

In short, according to postmodernism, humans not only cannot know the truth about reality but do not have the intellectual tools to do so because the language used to describe the reality is itself a linguistic construct which means that it is not objective. In view of this we should ask the question asked by Mark Lilla: "How should we understand the propositions of deconstruction? As more than one critic has pointed out, there is an irresolvable paradox in using language to assert that language cannot be used to make assertions that are not ambiguous."[142]

Denial of Personal Objectivity

"Whether the knower is conditioned by the particularity of his or her situation or not, theories are used oppressively, knowledge is not a neutral means of discovery."[143]

Denial of Certainty

"Knowledge is uncertain. Foundationalism, the idea that knowledge can be erected on some sort of bedrock of indubitable First principle, has had to be abandoned."[144]

Denial of Meta-Narrative

"All- inclusive systems of explanation, whether meta-physical or historical, are impossible, and the attempt to construct them should be abandoned...."[145]

Denial of Inherent Goodness of Knowledge

"The belief that by means of discovering the truths of nature it could be controlled and evils and ills overcome has been disproven by the destructive ends to which knowledge has been put (in warfare, for instance)...."[146]

Rejection of Progress

"Progress has been rejected. The history of the twentieth century should make this clear."[147]

Supremacy of Community-Based Knowledge

"The model of isolated individual knower as the ideal has been replaced by community-based knowledge. Truth is defined by the community, and all knowledge occurs within some community."[148]

Obviously, postmodernism is a reaction to the suppositions of modernism. This fact means that the Evangelical church of our day faces a challenge in ministering to persons who have been influenced by postmodernism. Understanding of the implications of Postmodernism is necessary for effective witness and ministry in this day.

Disbelief in the Objectivity

"The scientific method as the epitomization of the objective method of inquiry is called into question. Truth is not known simply through reason, but through other channels, such as intuition."[149]

This list includes only the most significant suppositions of the postmodern worldview. In our literature we have included books that discuss these in much more detail. In this next section we will discuss some of the barriers and some of the bridges for communicating the message of salvation to people with the postmodern worldview.

Barriers to Communication
With Postmoderns

What are the barriers and bridges to communicating the gospel message to people with a postmodern worldview? The reaction of postmoderns to the modern worldview applies to the methodologies that are employed in communicating the gospel message.

Rejection of Human Reason

Negative reactions will arise to a methodology that tries to use only human reasoning to convince people that they need to accept a number of prepositions to understand and receive salvation. If the modern worldview has much confidence in human reasoning and the presentation of the message of salvation reflects this, the message will be rejected simply because it is excessively identified with that worldview. The question that arises here is: To what extent is the influence of this worldview on the way modern Evangelicals present the gospel message a barrier to reach the postmodern?

Stanley J. Grenz argues that the evangelical movement is based on the Age of Enlightenment. He explains:

> The evangelical movement was born in the early modern period and in North America reached its highest point at the height of the modern period. Evangelicals are thinkers of modernism ... They have always used the tools of modernity, borrowing heavily from the scientific method. When evangelicals attempted to respond to the secularism of late modernism, these trends became especially evident. Much of their effort was devoted to an apologetic that would demonstrate the credibility of the "Christian faith to a culture that exalts reason and science.[150]

Erickson adds:

> Evangelicalism also is generally concerned about the propositional content of faith. Thus, its systematic theologies generally aim to provide a logical presentation of truth, a summary or synopsis of the themes of the teachings in Holy Scripture. That is because evangelicalism has defined itself in terms of a set of doctrines believed. A new paradigm for evangelicalism must be developed to fit this new and different situation... The younger generation, who take for granted the information age, MTV, and channel surfacing, are even more committed to the

postmodern vision of reality. This generation is not impressed as their predecessors with linear thinking, rational arguments and final answers. This is a clarion call to evangelicals to understand what is happening and to respond in the most appropriate way.[151]

The rejection of the metanarrative

There will be a backlash if the gospel message is presented as a metanarrative. If the purpose of presenting the gospel is that people accept a complete (Christian) worldview and the impression is given that it applies equally to all people of all cultures, there will be very little receptivity on the part of the postmodern.

Rejection of Focus on the Individual

If the emphasis of the presentation of the gospel is the certainty that religious suppositions about the individual (isolated from the community) can receive and understand truth there will be doubt on the part of postmoderns. The question arises to what extent has the evangelical movement been influenced by modern suppositions that base their approach and methodology on these rather than on the Bible itself. There is no denying that the personal and individual decision to receive Christ is a biblical basis. At the same time there are many examples of this type of decision made in the context of the family (eg., Cornelius, The Phillipian Jailer, Lydia, etc.)

It is important to be aware of the barriers that are in the minds of the part of postmoderns. The closer the communication of the gospel is to the suppositions of the modern worldview, the more resistance there will be on the part of the postmodernists. It should be noted however that although attention should be given to the way it presents the message of salvation, there are basic truths that cannot be ignored if the message is to be truly biblical. In the reflection section will give attention to this.

Bridges for Communication With Postmoderns

What are some of the bridges for communication of the gospel message to people with a postmodern worldview?

Brokenness of the modern mentality

The brokenness of the modern mentality (that has taken for granted that God is superfluous; that has failed to find a base for morality and society that has believed that progress is inevitable and that knowledge is inherently good) has opened the opportunity to demonstrate that in the postmodern world Christianity is intellectually relevant.[152]

Allen explains the relevance of Christianity:

> It is relevant to fundamental questions: Why does the world exist? Why does it have its present order rather than another? It is relevant to the discussion of the foundations of morality, society, especially on the significance to human beings. The recognition that Christianity is relevant to our entire society and relevant not only to the heart

but also to the mind, is a major change in our cultural situation.[153]

The breaking of the modern mentality opens up an opportunity to communicate the gospel message to people who have been influenced by postmodern thinking.

Spiritual Hunger

Although many of the postmodern worldview do not admit it, there is evidence that they have a deep spiritual hunger. This is made clear in the way Egleton describes the Western person:

> It has yearned for the sign which will give meaning to all others–the "transcendent signifier"–and for anchoring, unquestionable meaning to which all our signs can be seen to point (the "transcendental signified"). A great number of candidates for the role – God, the Idea, the World Spirit, the Self, substance, matter and so on – have thrust themselves forward from time to time.[154]

Although there is evidence of deep skepticism in the minds and hearts of the more extreme postmodernists (deconstructionists), the spiritual hunger that is reflected in their statements indicate that this can be a bridge to lead them to a personal experience with Christ, the true "transcendental signifier."

Importance of Community

Although we do not accept the supposition that truth can be known only individually but as a community, it is important to note that the postmodern worldview values the community. The Church can be that community in which the postmodern can see examples of divine truth in the lives of people and receive the transforming message of the gospel. The words of the Apostle Paul to the Thessalonians are instructive for us to minister to the Postmodern:

> [K]nowing, beloved brethren, your election by God. For our gospel did not come to you in Word only, but also in power, and in the Holy Spirit and in much assurance, as you know what kind of men we were among you.[155]

In his book, *Planting Churches in a Postmodern Age*, Ed Stetzer makes several suggestions to minister effectively to postmoderns in the context of Christian Communities.[156]

- First, being unashamedly spiritual. People have grown tired of the modern belief that everything can be answered by science and reason.

- Second, promoting incarnational ministry. Authenticity is essential, and authenticity only comes when we are real and present.

- Third, engaging in service. The key to engaging the postmodern passion is service.

- Fourth, valuing praise. Postmodern spirituality believes that our rational abilities are unable to grasp the whole truth and unable to provide the whole story.

- Fifth, preaching narrative expository messages. Postmoderns value the power of stories.

- Sixth, appreciating and participating in ancient patterns. Postmodern leaders are spellbound by the ancient-future faith of the past.

- Seventh, living in community. "Before the Church is called to do or say anything, it is called and sent to be the unique community of those who live under the reign of God... a form of companionship and wholeness that humanity craves" (Long, Generation Hope, 133-34).

- Leading transparent lives and as a team. Leadership in postmodern context tends to be dramatically different.[157]

Conclusion

We end this discussion of postmodernism with a recommendation made by Stanley Grenz and an admonition by Millard Erickson.

Grentz states that, " Evangelical theology must take on some of the characteristics of postmodernism if it is to minister effectively in this postmodern age."[158]

Erickson replies by affirming Grentz' statement while at the same time cautioning that Evangelical theology must not yield with regard to vital issues. For example, Erickson states that:

> [Evangelical Theology] must not give up the objectivity of truth to become irrational of anti-intellectual. It must not lose its emphasis on individual conversion and a personal relationship with Jesus Christ. It must resist the loss of all-encompassing truth. While recognizing that all views are culturally conditioned, it does not follow that all are equally valid. On the basis of their commitment to Jesus Christ and to the narrative based on God's action in him, evangelicals simply must reject the skepticism in much postmodernism. (Erickson, Postmodernizing, 100)

Reflection

Respond to suggestions made by Ed Stetzer for ministry in a postmodern context. With how many suggestions do you agree? Are there any with which you disagree? What changes would you make to this ministry plan?

1. Evaluate Stanley Grenz' statement above and the reply by Millard Erickson. With how many do you agree? What would you add to ensure that a postmodern oriented evangelical theology is genuinely biblical?

2. Evaluate David Wells' assessment of the influence the modern worldview when he sates: "As the nostrums of the therapeutic age supplant confession, and as preaching is psychologized, the meaning of the Christian faith became privatized. At a single stroke, confession is

eviscerated and reflection reduced to mainly thought about one's self."[159]

   a. Briefly evaluate the manner in which the pre-modern worldview has affected preaching in the context in which you live.

   b. Briefly evaluate the manner in which the modern worldview has affected preaching in the context in which you live.

   c. Briefly evaluate the manner in which the postmodern worldview has affected preaching in the context in which you live.

   d. Which of these worldviews has attracted more persons to the evangelical message in your region? Explain why.

3. If it is true that in the struggle against the liberalism the evangelical movement adopted the forms of modernism to defend and propagate its faith, what precautions should evangelicals take in our day to avoid falling in a similar situation in trying to communicate with postmoderns?

Bibliography

Allen, Diogenes. *Christian Belief In A Postmodern World*. Louisville, Kentucky: Westminster/John Knox Press, 1989

Best, Steven. Douglas Kellner, *Postmodern Theory*. New York: Blackwell, 1989.

Borgmann, Albert . *Crossing the Postmodern Divide*. Chicago: University of Chicago Press, 1992.

Burnham, Fredrick B. *Postmodern Theology* : *Christian Faith in a Pluralistic World*. San Francisco: Harper San Francisco, 1989.

Dockery, David S. ed., *The Challenge of Postmodernism: An Evangelical Engagement*. Wheaton, Illinois: Victor, 1995.

Giddens, Anthony. *The Consequences of Modernity*. Stanford, California: Stanford University Press, 1990.

Goizeuta, Roberto, "Rationality or Irrationality? Modernity, Postmodernism, and the US Hispanic Theologian," *Caminemos con Jesús: Toward a Hispanic/Latino Theology of Accompaniment*. Maryknoll, NY: Orbis Books, 1995.

Gonzalez, Justo, "Metamodern Aliens in Postmodern Jerusalem," *Hispanic/Latino Theology: Challenge and Promise*, ed. AM Isai-Diaz and FF Segovia, Minneapolis: Fortress Press, 1996.

Grenz, Stanley. *A Theology for the Community of God*. Nashville: Broadman & Holman, 1994.

_____. *A Primer on Postmodernism*. Grand Rapids: Eerdmans, 1996.

Phillips, Timothy R. and Okholm, Dennis L. *Apologetics in the Postmodern World*. Downers Grove, Ill: Intervarsity Press, 1995

Toulmin, Stephen. *Cosmopolis: The Hidden Agenda of Modernity*. New York: Free Press, 1990.

Wells, David. *The Person of Christ: A Biblical and Historical Analysis of the Incarnation*. Westchester, Ill: Crossway, 1984.

Conclusion

This has been a brief overview of worldviews that surround us in our ministry to reach the Latin American people with the message of salvation and establish congregations that are solidly biblical yet culturally relevant. This task is not an easy one due to the fact that there are concepts in the worldviews that we have presented that are completely against what the Word of God teaches. These mistaken concepts in the various worldviews are what constitute barriers to the communication of the gospel. At the same time, there are many concepts that can serve as bridges for evangelization.

It is my sincere hope that this review will stimulate us to devote more time to detailed study of the worldviews represented in the groups among whom we work. In addition to a literary study it will help to do a personal and local analysis to have a clearer idea of the individual worldviews and the basic suppositions that people have in the communities that surround us. Even though this will require much time and effort, it is absolutely necessary in order that people might truly understand the teachings of the Word of God and apply them to their lives personally and corporately in their congregations.

In our day there is a great need to design discipleship methods that take into account the person's worldview. This kind of discipleship must ensure that people understand clearly the basic doctrines of the Word of God and apply them to their daily lives. Such topics as prayer, reading God's Word, and worship are vital for new believers. In addition, however, contextualized discipleship must deal with the issues that people face in their daily lives. For example, in an animistic or syncretistic worldview setting, issues such as those listed here should be dealt with: consulting medicine men, evil eye, and veneration of saints, sacrifices, and other practices that hinder the spiritual growth of the new believers. This approach will not only help them in their personal lives but also equip them to live lives that give evidence of the power of the gospel to transform people and enable them to live victorious lives.

May the Lord bless you and guide you in this task.

To God be the glory.

APPENDIX A

God Loves Us
But Doesn't Like Us

We know that God loves us but don't understand why He doesn't like us.

We can see that He loves because He gave His only Son to die on a cross for us so that we could live and never have to die.

But, we have to learn to sing Christian music, play Christian instruments, dress in clothes of Christian culture, and sit in rows.

Everything must be done in the cultural style of the missionary.

The truth is that it confuses us that God apparently dislikes everything about our culture, while He loves us so much.

Statement by a member of a Native American tribe in the U.S.A.

APPENDIX B
Essential Beliefs
Concerning Salvation

1. There is only one God.
2. God is holy and just.
3. God is creator and governor.
4. God knows everything.
5. God can do everything.
6. God gives us what we need.
7. God speaks through His Word.
8. God keeps His promises
9. God hates sin and separates from it.
10. God punishes sin with death.
11. We can choose to sin against God.
12. We are responsible to God for what we do
13. We cannot do anything to escape the punishment of God
14. Only the perfect sacrifice of God can remove sin
15. Jesus is God's perfect sacrifice.
16. We are saved when we believe that Christ died in our place

Note: This list was designed by James Slack and J.O. Terry in an effort to clarify the biblical truths that are essential for a person to understand the concept of salvation.

The Whole Counsel of God

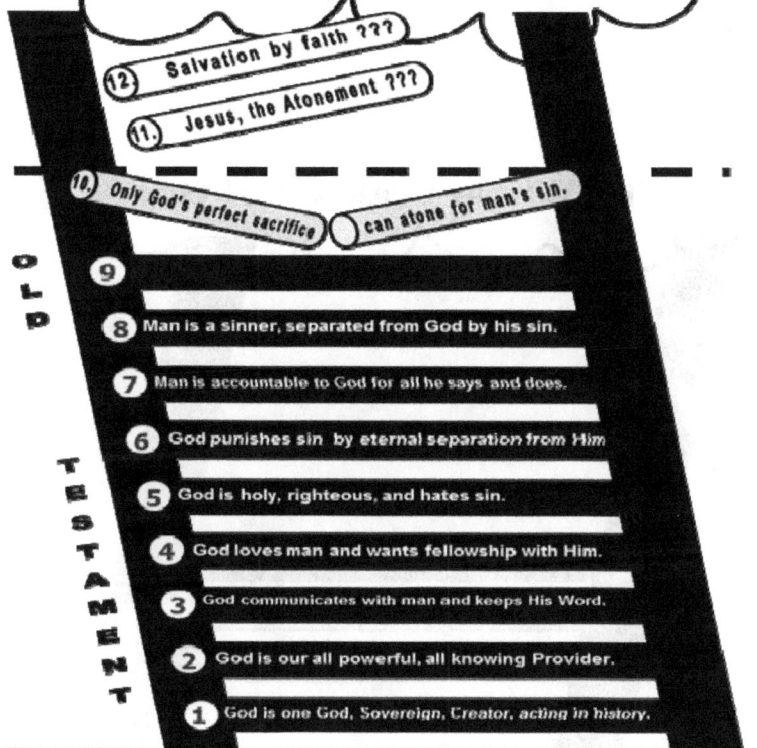

12. Salvation by faith ???

11. Jesus, the Atonement ???

10. Only God's perfect sacrifice can atone for man's sin.

OLD TESTAMENT

9.

8. Man is a sinner, separated from God by his sin.

7. Man is accountable to God for all he says and does.

6. God punishes sin by eternal separation from Him

5. God is holy, righteous, and hates sin.

4. God loves man and wants fellowship with Him.

3. God communicates with man and keeps His Word.

2. God is our all powerful, all knowing Provider.

1. God is one God, Sovereign, Creator, acting in history.

Jewish Worldview

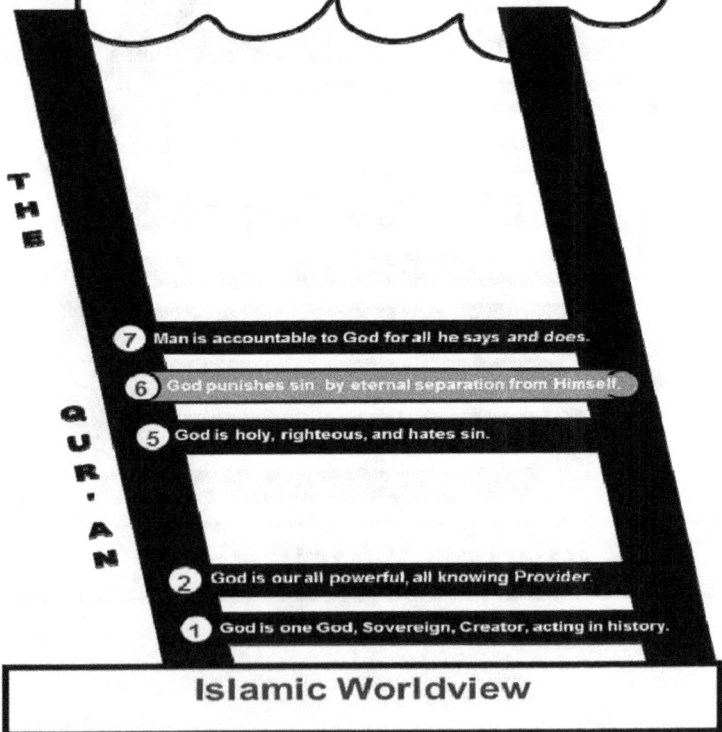

The Whole Counsel of God

THE

QUR'AN

⑦ Man is accountable to God for all he says and does.

⑥ God punishes sin by eternal separation from Himself.

⑤ God is holy, righteous, and hates sin.

② God is our all powerful, all knowing Provider.

① God is one God, Sovereign, Creator, acting in history.

Islamic Worldview

KINGDOM OF HEAVEN

PURGATORY

SUBSTITUTE — BELIEFS ???

13 ASSURANCE OF SALVATION.

SUBSTITUTE — BELIEFS ???

10 JESUS- ONLY MEDIATOR.

SUBSTITUTE — BELIEFS ???

6 SALVATION – FAITH IN CHRIST ALONE

SUBSTITUTE — BELIEFS ???

5 JESUS DIED ON THE CROSS.

3 JESUS WAS BORN OF THE VIRGIN MARY.

2 HOLY TRINITY

1 GOD- CREATOR OF UNIVERSE.

**SOLID & BROKEN RUNGS IN
ROMAN CATHOLIC LADDER**

APPENDIX C

Bridges and Barriers
In The Worldviews

BRIDGES

- Dreams

- Brokenness

- Testimonies

- Cultural Stories

- Moral and Spiritual Desire

- Receptivity to Communication Means

- Curiosity

- Prior Knowledge About God

- Redemptive Analogies

BARRIERS

- Ignorance

- Apathy

- Cultural Tradition

- Previous Beliefs and Practices

- Nominalism

- Fear of Persecution

- Fear of Losing Benefits and Social Materials

- Fear of losing harmony in the community

- Fear of disturbing the spirit world

- Incorrect Information about Christianity, Prejudices

Endnotes

Chapter 1

[1]Missiology – The science that studies the theology of missions, develops a philosophy of missions and proposes practical strategies for world missions as obedience to the Great Commission (Matt 28:19-20). Pablo Alberto Deiros, *Diccionario Hispano-Americano De La Misión* Box, Argentina: International COMIBAM, 1997

[2]Pablo Deiros, Diccionario Hispano de la Misión, Casilla, Argentina: COMIBAM Internacional, 1997.

[3]Charles H. Kraft, "Culture, and Contextualization," in, *Perspectives On The World Christian Movement*, eds. Ralph D. Winter, Steven C. Hawthorne (Pasadena: William Carey Library, 1999), 385.

[4]Kraft, Charles H., *Anthropology for Christian Witness*. New York: Orbis Books, 1996, 51.

[5]Hiebert, Paul G. and Meneses, Eloise Hiebert, *Incarnational Ministry: Planting Churches in Band, Tribal, Peasant, and Urban Societies*, Grand Rapids: Baker, 1995, 13 and 41.

[6]Ibid, 41-42.

[7]Wright, NT, *The New Testament And The People Of God* (Minneapolis: Fortress Press, 1992) 38

[8]Norman Geisler, "Some Philosophical Perspectives on Missionary Dialogue" in *Theology and Mission*, ed. David J. Hesselgrave. Grand Rapids: Baker Book House, 1978, 241-57.

[9]James W. Sire, *The Universe Next Door: A Basic Catalog*. Downers Grove: Intervarsity, 1997, 17.

[10] Etnic (gr. ethne, peoples). Race, people, cultural group; a natural group of individuals with common language and culture. The word is used in the Great Commission : (*ta ethne*). A sociological group of people large enough, they are aware that share a common link with each other (ethnicity, language, religion, occupation, class, caste, etc.). Paul Deiros, *Hispanic Dictionary of the Mission.*

[11]James W. Sire, *The Universe Next Door: A Basic Catalog*, 15.

[12]Copyright ©2003 by Gailyn Van Rheenen. Used by permission. All rights reserved.

[13]Ninian Smart, *Crosscultural Explorations of Human Belief*, Third Edition. (New York: Charles Scribner's Sons, 2000), 33, 34.

[14]Deiros defines inculturation as: 1. Transmission of culture from one generation to another within the same culture. 2. According to *DP:* «The transposing of the evangelical message anthropological language and to the symbols of the culture in which it is inserted.» Deiros, Pablo Alberto: *Diccionario Hispano-Americano De La Misión*, Casilla, Argentina : COMIBAM Internacional, 1997.

[15]This can include drastic changes on a personal, national, or global scale (E.g., tragedies, wars, invasions, drastic political changes, epidemics, etc.).

[16]De Carvalho, Levi: *Misión Global*, (Pasadena, California : Centro latinoamericano para la misión mundial, 2006), 226

[17]Hiebert, Paul G. and Meneses, Eloise Hiebert, *Incarnational Ministry: Planting Churches in Band, Tribal, Peasant, and Urban Societies,* 13 and 41-42.

[18]Ninian Smart, *Crosscultural Explorations of Human Belief* (New York: Charles Scribner's Sons, 1983), 2.

[19] Wright, N.T, *The New Testament And The People Of God* .

20Winter, Ralph & Hawthorne, Steven (Editors), Perspectives article "The Willowbank Report: The Lausanne Committee for World Evangelization," Pasadena: William Carey Press, 484.

[21]James B. Slack, "Why Fear", not published, March, 1999.
[22]Ibid.
[23]Ibid.

Chapter 2

24Gailyn Van Rheenen, *Communicating Christ in Animistic Contexts* (Pasadena, CA: William Carey Library, 1991), 25.
[25]Eugene A. Nida, and William A. Smalley, *Introducing Animism* (New York: Friendship Press, 1974), 5.
[26]Ibid, 51..
[27]Edward B. Taylor, *Primitive Culture*, 1871.
[28]Edward B. Taylor, *Religion in Primitive Culture (Primitive Culture* Part 2). (London: John Murray, 1958. Reprint, Gloucester, Mass: Peter Smith), 11.
[29]Ibid, 10.
[30]Deiros, Pablo Alberto: *Diccionario Hispano-Americano De La Misión.* 1997
[31]Gailyn Van Rheenen, *Communicating Christ in Animistic Contexts,* 20.
[32]Eugene A. Nida, William A. Smalley, *Introducing Animism,* 5.
[33]Douglas J. Hayward, "The Evangelization of Animists: Power, Truth or Love Encounter?" *International Journal of Frontier Missions* 14:4, Oct.-Dec. 1997: 155.
[34]Gailyn Van Rheenen, "Defining an Animistic," 2003.
[35]Nida and Smalley, *Introducing Animism* , 51.
[36]Ibid.
[37]Lausanne Occasional Papers, Number 16 Thailand Report, Christian Witness to Traditional Religionists of Asia and Oceania, 1980, 6.
[38]Lausanne Occasional Papers, Number 16 Thailand Report, Christian Witness to Traditional Religionists of Asia and Oceania, 1980, 5.
[39]Gailyn Van Rheenen, "Defining an Animistic," 2003.
[40] Nida and Smalley, *Introducing Animism,* 55.
[41]Ibid, 51.
43Philip Steyne, *Gods of Power: A Study of the Beliefs and Practices of Animist* (Houston: Touch Publications, 1990), 60.
[44]Gailyn Van Rheenen, "Defining an Animistic," 2003.
[45]Other suppositions of animism are a mystical view of life, a cyclical perspective of time and a ritualistic perspective of life..
[46]Paul G. Hiebert, "The Flaw Of The Excluded Middle," in Ralph Winter & Steven C. Hawthorn, *Perspectives on the World Christian Movement* (Pasadena: William Carey Library, 1999), 414-421.
[47]Ibid.
[48] lan Tippett, "The Evangelization of Animists," in Ralph D. Winter & Steven C. Hawthorn, *Perspectives on the World Christian Movement,* Pasadena: William Carey Library, 1999, 625.
[49]Alan Tippett, "The Evangelization of Animists," in Ralph D. Winter & Steven C. Hawthorn, *Perspectives on the World Christian Movement,* Pasadena: William Carey Library, 1999, 625. This is a brief summary of Tippett's article.
[50]Nida and Smalley, *Introducing Animism,* 56-58.
[51]There are those who prefer not to use the term "syncretism." Miguel de la Torre, for example, states that the members of an established religion utilize this term to give the impression that syncretism is an " impure religions" while theirs is "pure." Miguel A. De

La Torre, *Hispanic American Religious Cultures*, Volume Two, Santa Barbara: ABC CLIO, 2009, 540. This does not necessarily mean we cannot use this term. What it does mean is that we must be aware of this trend and be vigilant about syncretistic ideas that can be introduced in our Christian worldview. However, after accepting that warning we should be aware that this is not a matter of comparing one religion with another religion or to use this as a model to evaluate the others but of examining each in the light of Scripture.

Chapter 3

[52]Miguel A. De La Torre, *Hispanic American Religious Cultures*, Volume Two (Santa Barbara: ABC CLIO, 2009), 540.
[53]Alan R.Tippett, "Christopaganism or Indigenous Christianity" in *Christopaganism or Indigenous Christianity?* Tetsunao Yamammori and Charles Taber, eds., (Pasadena: William Carey Library, 1975), 32.
[54]ibid, 17.
[55] *Diccionario De La Lengua Española, Real Academia* Española, Vigésima Segunda Edición, 2001, 2069.
[56] Pablo Alberto Deiros, *Diccionario Hispano-Americano De La Misión*. 1997.
[57]Charles H. Kraft, "Culture and Contextualization," in, *Perspectives on the World Christian Movement*, ed Ralph D. Winter, Steven C. Hawthorne (Pasadena: William Carey, 1999), 390.
[58]Gailyn Van Rheenen, "Worldview and Syncretism," *Copyright ©2003 by Gailyn Van Rheenen. Used by permission. All rights reserved.*
[59]Willowbank Report, "Lausanne Committee," en Ralph D. Winter, Steven C. Hawthorne, *Perspectives on the World Christian Movement*, (Pasadena: William Carey, 1999), 394.
[60]Gailyn Van Rheenen, "Worldview and Syncretism," 4. *Copyright ©2003 by Gailyn Van Rheenen. Used by permission. All rights reserved.*
[61]Ibid.
[62]Charles H. Kraft, "Culture, and Contextualization," in, *Perspectives on the World Christian Movement*, 341.
[63]Gilberto Cavazos-González, "Religión Popular," in Miguel A. De La Torre, ed., *Hispanic American Religious Cultures*, Volume Two (Santa Barbara: ABC CLIO, 2009), 713.
[64]Ibid.
[65]Ibid.
[66]Vatican Council II, The Conciliar and Post Conciliar Documents, New York: Costello Publishing company, Inc., 1979, 421-22.
[67]Gilberto Cavazos-González, "Virgin Mary," en Miguel A. De La Torre, ed., *Hispanic American Religious Cultures*, Volume Two (Santa Barbara: ABC CLIO, 2009), 570.
[68]Néstor Medina, "Native Americans," in Miguel A. De La Torre, ed., *Hispanic American Religious Cultures,* Volume Two, Santa Barbara: ABC CLIO, 2009, 401
[69]Ibíd., 571-576
[70]Cited in David A Brancing, *La Virgen de Guadalupe: Imagen y Tradición* (México: Taurus, 2001), 9.
[71]Néstor Medina, "Native Americans," 401
[72]Ibid, 399-400.
[73]De La Torre, *Hispanic American Religious Cultures,* 540.
[74]It is known also in Cuba as the religion of Lucumí and the Regla de Ocha (Rule of the Saint) while in Brazil the same practice has the name of Candomblé. The African name of Santería is Ocha. Literally the name "santería" means worship of saints (*santos*). There are several African-American traditions, partly because of its reliance on oral traditions, as they do not have a holy book as a guide.

[75]Néstor Medina, "Santería," in Miguel de la Torre, ed., Hispanic American Religious Cultures, Volume Two, Santa Barbara: ABC CLIO, 2009, 506-7..
[76] The 16 are Elewá, Obatalá, Orunla, Changó, Ogún, Ochosi, Babalú-Ayé, Aganyú, Oricha-Oko, Inle, Osaín, Obba, Yemayá, Oyá, Ochún y los Ibeyi. The five orishas that make up the foundation of Santeria are Elewa, Obatala, Chango, Yemaya and Oshun.
[77]Donald T. Moore, "La Santería," VIII: 6, Nov.-dic., 1993: Dr. Donald T. Moore, Calle Jefferson 616, La Cumbre, Río Piedras, PR 00926.
[78]Ibid.
[79]Gailyn Van Rheenen, Worldview and Syncretism, *Used by permission. All rights reserved*
[80]Charles H. Kraft, "Culture, and Contextualization," in Ralph D. Winter, Steven C. Hawthorne, *Perspectives on the World Christian Movement*, 390.
[81]The other monotheistic worldview is Judaism.
[82]The groups of Christians in Arabia in that era were Orthodox, Coptics, and Nestorians. Muhammad mentions his contacts with Jews and Christians in the Surahs 14 and 15.

Chapter 4

[83]The Kur'an in 8:42 y 3:123 describes the approval and help of Allah in the victory. John L. Esposito, Darrell J. Fashing, Todd Lewis, World Religions of Today, Oxford: Oxford University Press, 2002, 191-193.
[84]*The Qur'an Translation*, Elmhurst, New York: Tahrike Tarsile Qur'an, Inc., 2007, 335-38.
[85]Ishak Ibraham, "Reaching Muslim People with the Gospel," in Ralph D. Winter, Steven Hawthorne, *Perspectives on the World Christian Movement*, (Pasadena: William Carey Library, 1999), 648
[86]Ibid.
[87]Samuel P. Schlorft, "Muslim Ideology and Christian Apologetics," in *Missiology: An International Review*, Volume XXI, Number 2, April, 1993, 175.
[88]Ibid.
[89]Ibid.
[90]The Spanish translation of the Qur'an translates the Arabic "Allah" with the Spanish word "Dios" which means "God" See *El Corán: El libro sagrado del Islám*, Madrid: Edimat Libros, 1998. Those quoting the Qur'an in Spanish, need to point out that they are not necessarily suggesting that the two words are to be used interchangeably.
[91]Ibid.
[92]Samuel Shahid, *The Cross or the Crescent: Understanding Islam* (Atlanta: North American Mission Board, 2001), 47
[93]Ibid., 176.
[94]These conclusions were given by Gerhard Nehls and Walter Eric, *Islam: As It Sees Itself, As Others See It, As It is* (Nairobi: Life Challenge Africa), 1996.
[95]Schlorft, 177..
[96]Taken from Fry & *King, Islam*, 1980, pp. 72-86.
[97]Ibid., 176,7.
[98]Charles H. Kraft, "Culture, and Contextualization," in Ralph D. Winter, Steven H. Hawthorne, *Perspectives on the World Christian Movement*, 1999, 390.
[99]Charles H. Kraft, *Anthropology for Christian Witness*, 67, 68.
[100]It is evident that Muhammad received this impression of "Christians," that belonged to the sects that had deviated from the Word of God.

[101]Warren Christian, "On The Turning of Muslim Stumbling Blocks into Stepping Stones," in Ralph D. Winter, Steven H. Hawthorne, *Perspective on the World Christian Movement,* (Pasadena: William Carey Library, 1999), 652.

[102]Ibíd. 652.

[103]George W. Braswell, Jr., *Guía Holman de Religiones del Mundo* (Nashville: B&H en Español, 200), 108.

[104]Bassam M. Chedid, *Islam: What Every Christian Should Know* (Webster, NY: Evangelical Press, 2004), 199

[105]Samuel Shahid, *The Cross or the Crescent: Understanding,* 47.

[106]Muslims believe that Jews and Christians corrupted the Bible so if there are differences Between the Bible and the Kur'an is it because the Bible has been corrupted. 2:106, 13:39, 16:101

[107]George W. Braswell, Jr., *Guía Holman de Religiones del Mundo* (Nashville: B&H en Español, 200), 108.

[108]Ibid., 108

[109]See Surah 23:102-104

[110]John Travis (un pseudonym), The C1 to C6 Spectrum, en Ralph D. Winter, Steven H. Hawthorne, *Perspectives on the World Christian Movement* , 1999, 658-9.

[111]External language is the one that persons who are not Muslims use. Internal language is used by Muslims.

Chapter 5

[112]David K. Naugle, *The History Of A Concept* (Grand Rapids: William Eerdmans Publishing Co., 2002), 174.

[113]Being that postmodernism defines worldview as a meta-narrative and believes that meta-narratives are not acceptable to explain reality, in a certain sense it is a contradiction of terms to say that there is a "Postmodern Worldview." However, it is interesting that in postmodernism there are suppositions that are accepted on a grand scale.

[114]David K. Naugle, *The History Of A Concept,* 186.

[115]Ibid., 173

[116]Millard J. Erickson, *Postmodernizing the Faith* (Grand Rapids: Baker Book House, 1998), 15.

[117]James W. Sire, *The Universe Next Door,* (Downers Grove, Illinois: InterVarsity Press, 2004), 26-44.

[118]David K. Naugle, 174

[119]Due to the limitations of time and space I have decided to use their brief and precise descriptions.

[120]Millard J. Erickson, *Postmodernizing the Faith,* 16.

[121]Ibid.

[122]Ibid.

[123]Ibid.

[124]Ibid, 17.

[125]Ibid.

[126]Ibid.

[127]Ibid.

[128]Ibid.

[129]Ibid.

[130]Ed Stetzer, *Planting New Churchesi in A Postmodern Age* (Nashville: Broadman & Holman Publishers, 2003), 119.

[131]David Wells cited in Ed Stetzer, *Planting New Churches In A Postmodern Age* (Nashville: Broadman & Holman Publishers, 2003), 119.

[132]Diogenes Allen, *Christian Belief in A Postmodern World,* Louisville, Kentucky: Westminster/John Knox Press, 1989, 2-5.

[133]James W. Sire, *The Universe Next Door,* 212.

[134]Ed Stetzer, *Planting New Churches in A Postmodern Age,* 119.

[135]Ibid.

[136]Jean-François Lyotard, *The Post Modern Condition: A Report on Knowledge* , trans. Geoff Benington and Brian Massumi, (Minneapolis: University Press, 1984), 24.

[137]James W. Sire, *The Universe Next Door,* 214

[138]Diogenes Allen, *Christian Belief In A Postmodern World,* 9.

[139]James W. Sire, *The Universe Next Door,* 214

[140]Ibid.

[141]Terry Egleton, Literary Theory, Minneapolis: University of Minnesota Press, 1983, 175.

[142]Mark Lilla, "The Politics of Jacques Derrida," New York Review of Books, June 25, 1998, 38.

[143]Millard J. Erickson, *Postmodernizing the Faith,* 18.

[144]Ibid.

[145]Ibid.

[146]Ibid.

[147]Ibid, 19.

[148]Ibid.

[149]Ibid.

[150]Stanley J. Grenz, "Star Trek and the Next Generation: Postmodernity and the Future of Evangelical Theology," in *The Challenge of Postmodernism: An Evangelical Engagement,* ed. David S. Dockery (Wheaton, Illinois: Victor, 1995), 90.

[151]Millard J. Erickson, *Postmodernizing the Faith,* 89.

[152]Diogenes Allen, *Christian Belief in A Postmodern World,* 2-5.

[153]Ibid, 5,6.

[154]Terry Egleton, *Literary Theory* (Minneapolis: University of Minnesota Press, 1988), 175.

[155]1 Thes 1:4-5.

[156]Ed Stetzer, *Planting New Churches In A Postmodern Age,* 137.

[157]Ibid, 137-155.

[158]Stanley J. Grenz, "Star Trek and the Next Generation: Postmodernity and the Future of Evangelical Theology," *in The Challenge of Postmodernism: An Evangelical Engagement,* 5, 90

[159]David Wells cited en Ed Stetzer, *Planting New Churches in A Postmodern Age,* 119

129